The Year at Great Dixter

Christopher Lloyd

—VIKING—

By the same author

The Well-Tempered Garden
Foliage Plants
The Adventurous Gardener
The Well-Chosen Garden

VIKING

Penguin Books Ltd, Harmondsworth, Middlesex, England
Viking Penguin Inc., 40 West 23rd Street, New York, New York 10010, U.S.A.
Penguin Books Australia Ltd, Ringwood, Victoria, Australia
Penguin Books Canada Limited, 2801 John Street, Markham, Ontario, Canada L3R 1B4
Penguin Books (N.Z.) Ltd, 182–190 Wairau Road, Auckland 10, New Zealand

First published 1987

Copyright © Christopher Lloyd, 1987

All rights reserved. Without limiting the rights under copyright
reserved above, no part of this publication may be reproduced, stored in
or introduced into a retrieval system, or transmitted, in any form
or by any means (electronic, mechanical, photocopying,
recording or otherwise), without the prior written permission of both
the copyright owner and the above publisher of this book

Designed by Yvonne Dedman

Typeset in Linotron Bembo
by Wyvern Typesetting Limited, Bristol
Printed in Spain by Graphicromo SA

British Library Cataloguing in Publication Data
Lloyd, Christopher, *1921–*
    The year at Great Dixter.
    1. Gardening
    I. Title   II. Toler, Pamela
    635   SB450.97

ISBN 0–670–80982–9

Frontispiece: The Barn and Sunk Gardens in July.

Contents

———◆———

Garden Plan of Great Dixter   6

Introduction
— 7 —

January
— 19 —

February
— 31 —

March
— 45 —

April
— 57 —

May
— 75 —

June
— 93 —

July
— 109 —

August
— 129 —

September
— 143 —

October
— 157 —

November
— 171 —

December
— 183 —

Index
— 189 —

Illustration Acknowledgements   192

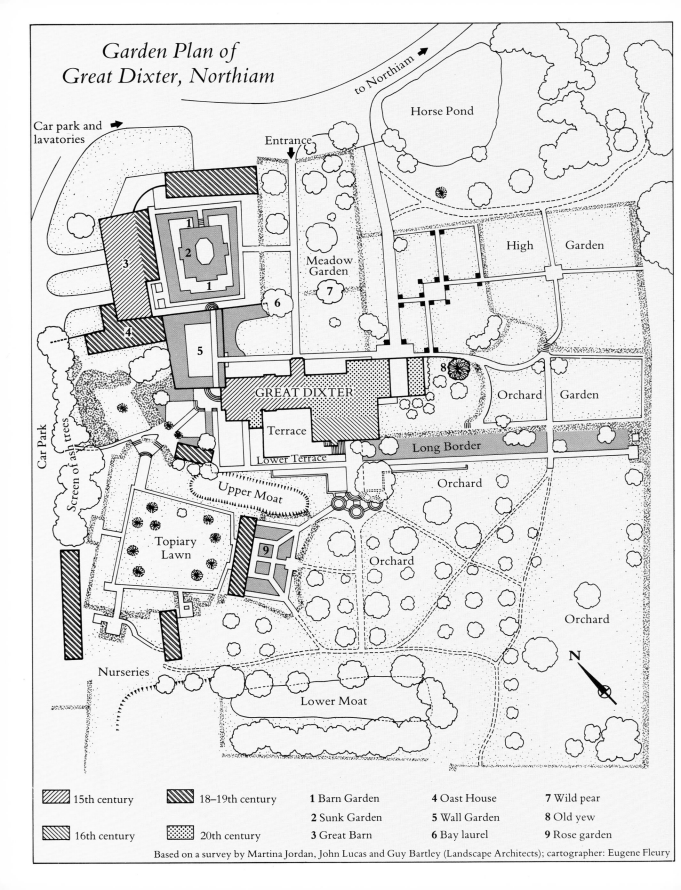

Garden Plan of Great Dixter, Northiam

Car park and lavatories

to Northiam

Horse Pond

Entrance

Meadow Garden

High   Garden

7

1

2

1

3

4

5

6

GREAT DIXTER

8

Orchard   Garden

Terrace

Long Border

Lower Terrace

Orchard

Upper Moat

Car Park

Screen of ash trees

Topiary Lawn

9

Orchard

Orchard

N

Nurseries

Lower Moat

▨ 15th century	◩ 18–19th century	**1** Barn Garden	**4** Oast House	**7** Wild pear
▨ 16th century	▦ 20th century	**2** Sunk Garden	**5** Wall Garden	**8** Old yew
		3 Great Barn	**6** Bay laurel	**9** Rose garden

Based on a survey by Martina Jordan, John Lucas and Guy Bartley (Landscape Architects); cartographer: Eugene Fleury

Introduction

————————◆————————

BEFORE launching into a garden's year, month by month, there is a clear duty to explain what and where Great Dixter is and why I should be writing about it at book length. In fact I have already been writing about it these thirty-four years (one third of a century – what a thought), directly or indirectly, since my first article on gardening (on my favourite *Lobelia cardinalis*) was published in the now defunct monthly magazine *Gardening Illustrated*.

I am one of those once common, now rare, people who still, at sixty-five, lives in the house where he was born (it wasn't even normal to be born in hospital, in those days). It can't go on much longer but it has been a good experience while it has lasted.

My parents bought Dixter, as it was then called (they added the Great to distinguish it more certainly from Little Dixter, which they also bought) and as I always think of it, in 1910, and my father engaged Edwin Lutyens to make the restorations and additions and to design the garden.

Dixter, a manor house, is a large timber-framed building constructed around 1460 and situated in the high weald. The weald of Kent and Sussex (German: *wald*, a wood) lies between the chalk of the North and South Downs, in south-east England, and the high weald is the centre part of this area.

Luckily for us, Dixter was sited on a south-west-facing slope 180 ft above sea level (the sea being some ten miles distant), and although not very high it is near the top of its hill and commands all-round views (once you have stepped outside the garden) in every direction except east. The land slopes down to the Rother valley. The Rother itself, where it forms the boundary to our property (and between Sussex and Kent) was tidal as I first remember it. The valley, as is the way of valleys, attracts frost and fog. It is marvellous to be perched above all that. On the other hand we are, or were, exposed to wind from most directions. Wind is a great enemy to gardening, and we have blithely planted out our views with trees and hedges so that wind damage has been considerably mitigated. Yet we are still close enough to the sea to experience a markedly kinder climate than, say, Sissinghurst Castle, which

My mother, Daisy Lloyd, trug on arm, in front of the porch at Great Dixter
in the 1960s. The original manor house was built around 1460.

also stands on a hill and is only eleven miles distant by road, but is just that much further inland to register a palpable climatic difference.

The whole of the weald was at one time covered with oak forest (it is still well wooded and the woods are crammed with primroses, anemones and bluebells in the spring). There is little suitable building stone just where we are, so nearly all the houses were built of oak, infilled with lath and plaster, and those of any size belonging to our period were hall houses. Our Great Hall is a large room made for communal living, open from floor to roof and from outside wall to outside wall. The large oak beam tying these walls is 35 ft long.

But when in Tudor times the fashion changed to smaller rooms and greater privacy, our hall (with all others like it) was filled in with two extra floors and numerous partitions. Other rooms were similarly treated. Lutyens restored the building to the *status quo ante* as far as was reasonable for a more comfortable and modern style of living and without resorting to too much guesswork where the evidence was no longer extant.

This lost the building much floor space, so two principal additions were made. Another, smaller, hall house, dated about 1500, was to be destroyed

My father, Nathaniel Lloyd. *Left*: with my eldest brother Selwyn
in the old Swift car. *Right*: at his drawing board in the study.

by its owner at Benenden, nine miles distant. My father bought it for very little, its beams were all numbered, and it was moved to Dixter and re-created. The other new wing built on was entirely of Lutyens's design, but working in the vernacular so as to marry discreetly with the original.

There was virtually no garden at Dixter in 1910. The property had in any case been on the agent's books for the past ten years – as 'an agricultural property with farmhouse attached' – and was occupied only by a summer tenant during that period. There were two orchards – the trees planted along ridges which show that the land had once been ploughed in the old style – and a few odd trees besides. A bay laurel, a wild pear and a fig survive. But there were farm buildings – a barn (possibly as old as Dixter itself) and oast house (dating from 1890 or so), a thatched (now shingled) stable unit, and cow houses, locally known as hovels. Also two round and two rectangular brick cattle drinking tanks. All these were ornamental; Lutyens saw how invaluable they would be as framework and ingredients in a new garden, so they were all worked into his design.

The gardens lie around the house, which is roughly in their centre, so that you have only to walk around the building to have made the garden circuit. It

Accurate yew hedge cutting in the early days.
Compare the old pear tree in the background with its present appearance *(p. 78)*.

is a satisfyingly intimate arrangement. If you want to dash out to pick some *Iris stylosa* buds or some sprigs of witch hazel or a bunch of lilies-of-the-valley or a last minute lettuce or bowl of raspberries, you can choose a door of exit so that nothing is far from your starting point.

Lutyens designed the garden walls and how the hedges should run, but my father had a great interest in topiary and he oversaw the planting, training and care of the yew and box hedges and of the many topiary pieces in various forms. Based on his experiences, mainly gained at Dixter, he wrote a book that is still useful, if you can get hold of it: *Garden Craftsmanship in Yew and Box*, published in 1923. In later editions of *The English Flower Garden*, William Robinson, who loathed topiary, made a snide reference to its use in Northiam, for it was also notable at Brickwall, at the other end of our village.

My father was originally a colour printer and founded his business, Nathaniel Lloyd and Co., in Blackfriars. But he gave this up on coming to live at Dixter (he was forty-four in 1910) and trained himself to be an architect (in a small way) and, more importantly, an architectural historian and also a photographer of buildings. Two of his major works are still in print.

Apart from the topiary, his main contribution to the gardens was in the Sunk Garden, made in 1923. It has an octagonal pool surrounded by flagstone paving, then dry walling up to grass slopes (beasts to mow), and so to the

The view east to Higham, our nearest neighbours, at 7.30 p.m. on 2 June after a cold storm. The High Garden and the top of the big yew are in the foreground.

garden's main level, the framework being barns on two sides, a Lutyens wall and yew hedging on the third and fourth. Originally there was just a farm track across this area. It is a scene of great repose. Wherever you stand there is a pleasing prospect across to features, including plantings, on the further side. The area is not large and visitors relate easily to it. 'If I could have just one piece of your garden it would be this,' they tell me, for it seems to be complete in itself. I say 'seems to be' because there has, in fact, to be a back-up area in which plants for different seasons can be raised and grown on. The gardens throughout consist of mixed borders where annuals and bedding plants are worked in (rather than given beds to themselves) among or in front of more permanent shrubs and perennials.

With his architect's eye for strong design, my father originally planted the four corners of the quadrangular Barn Garden (above and surrounding the Sunk Garden) with *Yucca gloriosa*. And the corner bed surrounding each yucca was planted with bearded irises. The theme was of spear and sword leaves. My mother, who was my great gardening influence and inspiration, was a plantswoman. She loved plants for their own sake. She did not love the yuccas, because of the danger to her children (six of us) and to everyone else from those sharp points. After my father died in 1933, the yuccas went. She replaced them with four *Malus sargentii*. She'd fallen for them at a Chelsea

Probably taken in spring, 1938, when I was seventeen and my mother fifty-seven.
After her first visit to Austria in 1936, she wore Austrian dirndl costume for the rest of
her life. My sister, Letitia, and the cocker spaniel Bunch are in the foreground.

Flower Show exhibit. This is seldom a sound basis for an important choice. The shrubs grew very large. They had no particular shape, their fruits are minute, and so they gave only a week of pleasure in the year and made no kind of unifying impact in their important positions.

She didn't like me for replacing them, in 1950, with *Osmanthus delavayi* (from Marchant's, in Dorset), but she did come to like the replacements very much indeed. Apart from their April flowering, they are comely evergreen shrubs (clipped annually) with neat little leaves, but I have to admit that, year-round, *Yucca gloriosa*, properly looked after with its dead leaves pulled off, would look better. I would not replace the irises. The bearded kinds look sordid for far too much of the year, and there is no way to disguise them as their rhizomes require a summer baking. My mother doted on irises and used to accept gifts of bearded varieties which, in bloom, swept her off her feet. This made me cross, and she had to grow them in spare corners where they did not interfere with the garden proper. They have no place in that at all.

When you have two strong-willed people working in the same garden (my mother died only in 1972 and was active till the last ten days of her ninety-one years) there are sure to be many clashes, and there were. But, as we loved each other, our shared pleasures in the garden were by far the strongest element in this partnership.

Gertrude Jekyll never had anything to do with the planting of the garden, contrary to what was stated in Betty Massingham's biography and has frequently been repeated since. I think my mother was quite probably the cause of the misconception. Towards the end of her life she used to imagine that what she would have liked to have been, had been, and she may have told Betty what she herself wanted and had come to believe. But there is no shred of evidence of Miss Jekyll's involvement, no plants, no letters. My parents did visit her at Munstead on at least two occasions, and I, as a small boy, very impressed, was there on one of them. Miss Jekyll blessed me and hoped that I would grow up to be a great gardener. I don't think I've imagined that!

The original planting of the borders was planned by Sir George Thorold, a member of the old Lincolnshire family. Clearly he was under the Jekyll influence, as evidenced, for instance, by large corner blocks of *Bergenia* (*Megasea*) *cordifolia*.

However, my mother's gardening bible was *The English Flower Garden*, and never mind what Robinson thought about topiary. Our battered, back-broken edition, with 'N. Lloyd' inscribed on the first page in my father's hand, was published in 1906 (my parents were married in '05) and it is larded with bookmarkers. It may have been from this that my parents took their dislike of statuary in the garden (there has never been a piece of sculpture at Dixter, but nothing is for ever . . .), though I think a presbyterian upbringing was a far more likely and earlier influence.

My mother's taste for wild gardening, especially in rough grass, was probably derived from Robinson, and also the manner of planting that he recommended. Our principal orchard, adjoining the Long Border (I love that conjunction of highly organized border and tall meadow grasses with only a path and a strip of mown grass dividing them), was planted with such daffodils and narcissi as were fashionable in those pre-war years (other gardens including the same varieties can be identified as having been created at the same period). Robinson wrote proudly of his own plantings that they throve and that 'the flowers are large and handsome, and in most cases have not diminished in size'. Fortunately his innate vulgarity with its biggest-is-best standards was only gratified, in those days, by flowers of what we should now consider very modest proportions (perhaps he would have disliked the

The view from the terrace, with *Magnolia soulangiana* 'Lennei' in the foreground, across the drained Upper Moat to the Topiary Garden.

modern monsters as much as I do), and so it is at Dixter in the orchard. But what is so pleasing here is that perhaps only one third of the area, if as much, is planted up with daffodils. The rest is left as turf (wherein earlier flowering snowdrops and crocuses also find a place). So there is no feeling of over-crowding or showing off. This spontaneous treatment was Robinson's recommendation. 'To scatter Narcissi equally over the grass everywhere is to destroy all chance of repose, of relief, and of seeing them in the ways in which they often arrange themselves.' You can take hints from the sky. 'Often a small cloud passing in the sky will give a very good form for a group, and be instructive even in being closer and more solid towards its centre, as groups of Narcissi in the grass should often be', and as ours are.

But the main fun my mother had with her meadow gardening was elsewhere, and was more likely based, I should guess, on what she'd seen in other gardens or in the wild, as well as including her own experiments of what might do in turf. The Upper Moat, drained on our arrival to form a piece of turf in the shape of a bath, was her principal scene of action in the early days. Here she started growing snakeshead fritillaries, which she used to raise from seed sown in boxes, pricked out into more boxes and then planted out with a bulb planter (a marvellous implement still going strong) and a trugful of potting soil. She also established, here, polyanthus that had previously been used for spring bedding. They have lasted so well that they form an interesting record of the appearance of these florist's flowers sixty and more years ago. I .remember her adding *Anemone apennina* to her tapestry, and many more things, including *Orchis mascula*, but there were no narcissi here at all.

Nor in front of the house, apart from Lent lilies, *Narcissus pseudonarcissus*, of which she was originally given stock from Beckley or Peasmarsh where, only a few miles distant from Northiam, they grow wild. I suspect that they came from the garden of a close friend, Molly Liddell, at Place House, Peasmarsh. Anyway, from small beginnings my mother increased them from seed, as she did the fritillaries, and after that they sowed themselves.

One other, taller narcissus in this front meadow, with small cupped yellow flowers, was given us by a Swiss governess of mine under the impression that they were the wild *Narcissus poeticus*. Great was our annoyance when they turned out to be nothing of the sort, but we never got rid of them.

This meadow flanks the front path on either side as you approach the porch and many visitors, since it is surrounded by trim yew hedges, think that lawns must have become neglected from shortage of labour, whereas actually wild gardening was intended here from the first.

There is another such small area, similarly puzzling to the public, going right up to the south-east end of the house. Planted with lilacs in poorly draining clay soil which they barely tolerate, it is notable chiefly for its display of goldilocks (*Ranunculus auricomus*), lady's smock and wood anemones, in spring, which no one wittingly introduced though they could hardly be improved upon.

The area round the Horse Pond, including the pond itself, was originally iron ore workings made when the local iron industry flourished. The excavations terminated at a steep bank, on which my brother Oliver planted birch and aspen saplings collected from one of our woods in the 1930s. Between this and the approach drive (called the forstal) are a number of fifty-year-old oaks which were self-sown seedlings at a time when, following my father's death, this area was neglected and filled with brambles, broom and rabbits. We subsequently cleaned it up and I have planted rhododendrons here, as well as smaller things that enjoy the shade of trees.

The Horse Pond is so called because the farm horses used to be led into it to drink and wallow at the end of their working day. It is a water garden now, and the grassy banks overlooking it are a particularly pleasant place of relaxation where I and my less formal friends (the majority) bring our coffee after lunch and enjoy the busy life that is conducted in and around a pond by birds, fish, snakes, frogs, toads, insects and other forms of life. There are a few relic heathers (*Calluna vulgaris*) here, improbably reaching out into the pond. My father planted two large patches of them and of gorse, which he called whins, out of sentiment. His mother was a Scot and he was brought up in Scotland.

My own interest in the garden goes back as far as I can remember, and it was encouraged by both my parents. In 1947, after demobilization, I studied horticulture at Wye College (University of London) in Kent and took a degree. Then I spent the next four years teaching there, after Miss Page, the lecturer in decorative (now called 'amenity', of all horrible words) horti-culture, fell seriously ill. This gave me just the scientific and practical training I needed to make me feel at home in my subject. Wye is only twenty-five miles from Dixter, so I was able to spend one or two days a week in my garden through this period while leaving my mother a list of instructions for the days when I was away. In the meantime my brother Quentin looked after (and still looks after) the estate and all matters pertaining to opening to the public.

In 1954 I returned home for good and started a nursery devoted to the kinds of plants, many of them unusual, which I like to grow in the garden. We sell to visitors on the spot, in the main, but mail orders account for perhaps a quarter of the business. I never intended it to become the tail that wags the dog because the enjoyment from a business of this kind arises from being able to handle much of it yourself, with all the personal contacts with like-minded people that this entails. Most of my friends have been made in this way and it has been a rewarding life.

The gardens were so well designed that I haven't needed to make major alterations to them. True, they are labour-intensive. We have three full-time gardeners and three or four part-timers. High maintenance gardening is the most interesting. This is a plantsman's garden and there are a great many plants I want to grow. Some look after themselves to a large extent and allow extra time for looking after the more exacting. But I never take on a plant *because* it will save me trouble nor, for that matter, because it will make heavy demands on me. I grow it because I like it and want to make it happy.

My great good fortune has been in opportunity and in the fact that I have been able to turn my consuming interest in plants and gardening and my enjoyment in writing to professional account. This is what has enabled me to make my life at Dixter. Taxation makes it unlikely that the situation can last much longer. His children were all heirs to my father's estate and as each of us dies off it becomes more difficult to pay that one's share of Capital Transfer Tax. It is a familiar situation. My ideal would be to be able to live my life out at Dixter for as long as my health lasts.

In the meantime I live happily. Although I am the only one permanently resident at Dixter, I do not feel I rattle around in it, as strangers are apt to suppose. I like being alone, with Tulipa my dachshund, when there's a book to write, but I also like to have friends to stay and I have had many such, particularly since I took to and found I enjoyed cooking, within the last eight or ten years. The fact that my brother and sister-in-law live close at hand at Little Dixter is also very sustaining. Our efforts are complementary.

The reason I want to write this book about the garden is because Dixter is a happy, if impermanent, microcosm. It has given and still gives pleasure to many people beyond my family, and I hope that I can communicate wherein these pleasures and the interests they arouse consist, not just in the summer but in every month of the year.

Christopher Lloyd

January

————————◆————————

I N *every* month of the year, did I say? 'I could do without January,' wrote Rosemary Verey in her *Country Life* notes. Most of us have that feeling about the grimmest month. On the human level we are in the reality of post-Christmas depression, bills flooding in (though the Inland Revenue cannily present theirs before the holiday) and nothing left in the kitty. Worries over health and heating beset us and the weather is a constant threat. I know there are those who say they love the winter and witter on about its crispness and sparkle and the inspiration of your breath hanging on the frosty air (not to mention the dewdrop on the end of your snotty nose), but on how many days in January do you actually see the sun? Most of the time you seem to be closed in by a weight of low, grey cloud so that it is half dark even at midday.

Not all the time. There are moments of relief, and nothing in a garden stays still for long, not in our maritime climate, not even in January.

You don't have to wait for a mild season to have *Iris histrioides* 'Major' in full bloom at some time this month. Although only a few inches high at flowering, which it does before the leaves extend, it makes a lively blue show and is amazingly tough. Not so tough, however, that the slugs won't eat it or sparrows behead the buds just as they are opening. In a garden the size of mine, plants the size of this tend to get lost or else they are forgotten at the very moment when they need to be remembered. If I had terraced rock ledges, that would be ideal for small things and it would give them the chance to be seen close to eye level. As it is, I find the best plan is to grow them in pans in a perfectly cold frame which is only covered by glass if there is danger from excess rain. But in any case my pans are all clay (the old hand-thrown ones are much the most solid and frost-resistant) and so they dry out again faster than would plastic containers.

When flower buds appear, I bring the pans indoors and enjoy their flowering (which lasts only a week in a warmish room but two if it's unliveably cold) on a table or window ledge. Then back to the cold frame. It's

Opposite: Topiary in fog;
looming in the background, the north side of Great Dixter.

Iris winogradowii lends itself ideally to being grown in a pan in a cold frame,
from which it can be brought indoors when flowering.

the same with *I. winogradowii*, which is similar to *histrioides* but primrose
yellow, flowering two or three weeks later so that its season runs on into
February. This species, whose price, reflecting its availability, has always
been prohibitive, is really a lot easier to manage, over a period, than the
popular, bright yellow *I. danfordiae*. In the latter, the bulb breaks up after
flowering into a number of tinies which then take two or three years to reach
flowering size again. In *I. winogradowii* this is not the case. There is never a
shortage of flowering-sized bulbs although they also breed plenty of spawn,
which can be grown on to flower in a couple of years.

There won't be room in my June chapter to mention these bulbs again and,
indeed, it is quite difficult to remember them at that time, but by late June
growth will have been completed. The dormant period is short, so I make a
note in my diary to turn the bulbs out and sort and grade them. I shake them
in a bag with a little Benlate (Benomyl) against ink spot disease, then repot
the large ones in pans and dibble the small ones into deep boxes for growing
on. The bulbs shrivel quite quickly if left out of moist soil, so it is a mistake to
dry them off for any length of time.

Another early flower that I grow in pans and which is generally in bloom (though it has a long season) by mid-month is *Anemone hortensis*. Despite its name suggesting a garden origin, this is a wilding, my stock having come, through a friend, from Tuscany. The colour is bright purple, with even a hint of magenta. I'm uncertain whether this is in commerce but the St Bavo strain, in mixed shades, is of the same style.

The frame in which I grow these and later-flowering bulbs abuts on the sunny side of the greenhouse, which itself has solid brick walls. I much prefer this arrangement to the standard patterns which have glass down to ground level. They heat up quickly in the sun but become desperately cold and unprotective at night.

My greenhouse is not a conservatory. Its chief role in winter is to hold rooted cuttings like fuchsias, felicias, gazanias, *Helichrysum petiolatum*, 'geraniums' and other slightly tender perennials in good health until they can be potted individually in the spring and transferred to cold frames. It has benches all round and a narrow alley between, while under the staging are stored or stacked a number of dormant plants as well as others, like *Zantedeschia aethiopica*, the greenhouse arum, whose light intensity requirements are low.

I do grow some fun plants as well, such as *Tropaeolum tricolorum*, the florist's genista and *Gladiolus tristis*, which grows in winter and is already 2 ft tall. But none of these are yet in flower. Everything is leafy and we spray weekly with a protective fungicide (varying the ingredient to prevent resistant botrytis strains from developing) so that the prevailing low temperatures do not bring on epidemics by fungus diseases, as can so easily happen, especially with woolly-leaved perennials such as gazanias.

The burning question is always: how low can we keep the greenhouse heating without running into trouble? Much lower than most people suspect, unless you're deliberately going in for tropical plants. My plants will nearly all spend a good slice of their year unprotected in the garden. They are not so very tender.

My ideal is that the temperature shall remain above freezing but only just. With fine tuning of that kind plans can easily go agley. So we have two sources of heat, both thermostat controlled, the less popular one coming on at a lower temperature than the other and acting in a supporting role. Electricity is the first line of defence, calor gas the second. The trouble with gas or paraffin or candles, or any other combustible heat source whose fumes are contained within the greenhouse instead of being channelled out of it by way of a flue, is that a great deal of harm can be done to your plants. Their growth takes on a crumpled, brittle, stunted look. The woolly-leaved *Helichrysum petiolatum* is especially susceptible and a good indicator. If its leaves start marginal browning I know I'm in trouble. So we fall back on the gas as little as possible but are especially glad of it when there's a power cut, which can easily happen in winter when supply cables are weighed down and broken by ice. In most winters my greenhouse fuel bills are remarkably low, but then, as I said at the start, I do live in a mildish part of Sussex and on a south-west-facing slope.

My cold frames (none are heated) are all pretty snug, having solid brick or 2-inch concrete walls. To date they are still covered with glass, which offers better protection than polythene though it is heavy to handle – we take it off and stack it whenever we can. But when heavy frosts are on, so is the glass and also a roll of hessian at night. It stays on by day, also, when there's snow, and this cosy situation can last for several weeks at a time, the plants in total darkness. That doesn't matter at low temperatures when even the evergreens cannot make use of light anyway. As soon as temperatures rise, off come the wraps and the lights and a fungicide spray is applied to any soft material that might otherwise succumb to the grey mould fungus.

A number of flowering shrubs are at their best in the outside winter garden, notably the Chinese witch hazel, *Hamamelis mollis*, whose flowers, incredibly, seem impervious to frost. And they are strongly scented on the air whenever temperatures rise a little. Two large specimens of the usual deep yellow kind were planted in the 1930s. They can never become all that large, as I plunder branches of them heavily for the house and they do not readily break with young shoots from old wood.

As they are invariably grafted on the seedlings of the American *H. virginiana*, you should treat those promising young shoots that arise from low down with suspicion. One of our bushes does sucker from the stock and I devote a session to removing them every other year.

Showier than *H. mollis* itself is the clone 'Pallida'. In this the ribbon-like petals are half as long again and, being a lighter and more luminous shade, they show up much more readily at a distance. My specimen of this is young and I cannot hack at it, which is frustrating. I think I must try and speed its growth with a good mulch of garden compost. We give our witch hazels a dressing of wood ash from the fireplaces from time to time, as they do otherwise suffer from potash deficiency, which shows up in summer as marginal leaf scorch.

Of winter sweet, *Chimonanthus praecox*, I now have six specimens, all different clones; three of them are seedlings, three grafted plants which are

A flower arrangement that I keep going through the winter, with berried branches
of *Celastrus orbiculatus* dominant. In January I can add winter sweet and Chinese
witch hazel, which scent the Great Hall as one scurries through to somewhere warmer.

much more precocious and will start flowering quite young. Seedlings may take six or seven years, and then their flowers may be so wee as to be hardly worth while, even given their delicious spicy scent (present also in the wood and roots, as you'll notice when handling them). Still, I have some good seedlings and they flower really freely in more years than not, but especially following a hot summer. It takes quite a heavy frost to damage the blooms, and then there'll always be further buds to take their place, so the protection of a warm wall is by no means essential unless yours is a dismal climate, even in summer. In that case I should give chimonanthus a miss.

Lonicera × *purpusii* will have carried a few early blooms, but makes a serious showing this month and next and it forces without coaxing, in water, indoors. It has very heavily scented white flowers with the somewhat sickly sweetness of *Lonicera japonica* 'Halliana' in the other half of the year. But *L.* × *purpusii* is a bush. I prune it by thinning out old branches and leaving the new untouched. It can be kept reasonably comely but should not be given a place of prominence. Luckily its leaves are shed before flowering commences. Its flowers are showier and freer than either of its parents, though I still have *L. fragrantissima*, since it is evergreen and fills a gap under my winter cherry, but it only flowers well after an exceptionally hot summer and even then the blossom is overpowered by its leaves.

Any sweet scent is welcome in winter, even when the quality (as in winter heliotrope, but that terrifying weed will never find a place at Dixter, I hope) is sickly. And so it is with the several available species of *Sarcococca*, whose season starts mid-month. I never feel I do these as well as I should, though my Dutch friend, Romke van de Kaa, assures me that they are always slightly scruffy. I'm afraid that's not entirely true, however, as I have seen them looking happier in your garden. I have four species, now, the four usuals, and still hope to please them unreservedly. Certainly they don't like to be blazed upon in full sun. Their evergreen leaves are neat and glossy and the small, white flowers seem, with all their modesty, entirely appropriate to the season.

I feel no deprivation in winter from being unable to draw upon the kind of hothouse flowers that would be available to me given properly heated glass maintaining an extravagant minimum temperature of 50 degrees F. There is always so much to bring into the house straight from the garden itself, and these sprigs, often scented, mean a great deal more than flabby florist's tulips or irises or, a recent fad, those wretchedly deformed forced lilies.

But most of the winter-flowering shrubs (including heathers) are rather dowdy when not in bloom, so I think it's a mistake to grow them all near the house, in a special winter gathering. In the summer, if not actually an eyesore, you'll be aware of the fact that they're not contributing, so I believe in scattering them around and perhaps growing a clematis through any of the larger specimens so as to mitigate their off-season dullness.

I have lately given up *Garrya elliptica*, whose grey-green catkins expand to their full length in January, weather permitting. I have never been without it since I can remember, and at its best it is very good indeed, so please go on growing it and let me admire your specimen in the right week of the year. I shall never grow it again. There's too much of the time that I find myself resenting its appearance. Even at flowering its catkins are not frost-proof, and if they're caught, they're all caught and there's nothing but the shrivelled remains to sustain you for another season.

How much better, even though it does not noticeably flower, the neighbour which, I think, finally shaded out my last garrya. This is *Daphniphyllum macropodum*, and no sort of weather that I have seen deters it. Its elliptical evergreen leaves (sometimes mistaken for a rhododendron's) grow in bouquets. They are glaucous on their undersides, while the stalk and main vein are bright carmine pink – a cheerful sight.

Another evergreen that I find full of cheer at this season is the clone of *Euonymus fortunei* called 'Emerald Gaiety'. It makes a comely single specimen to 3 ft or so, not over-large but not desperately slow-growing either. Its rounded leaves are variegated in green and white and this again is admirable to pick.

So, as all flower arrangers will know, is the marbled foliage of *Arum italicum* 'Pictum'. It is a hardy perennial that rests in summer. Growth is resumed in autumn, and from now till late spring it becomes increasingly luxuriant. I think that its pale veining goes especially well, in a bunch, with some of the larger snowdrops that will be at their peak next month.

Meanwhile I have to make preparations for them. One of the earliest, and usually in flower by mid-January even in a shady border, is the clone of *Galanthus nivalis* (the common snowdrop) called 'Atkinsii'. That I have growing in a wet spot between colonies of *Euphorbia palustris*. On the whole I don't bother to tidy my borders until March, but here is a case where the old stems of the spurge must be cut down so as to leave the snowdrop in full possession.

Likewise among the male ferns, which were finally frosted at the turn of the year and reduced to a state of sprawling collapse. There are snowdrops (there should be even more) among them and they must be released. Where I have them among hardy fuchsias the fuchsia stems must be removed. I know

Helleborus 'Atrorubens' usually opens its first blooms by Christmas.
Note Lutyens's decorative use of tiles in the paving beneath an archway.

that, traditionally, one waits till spring before pruning less hardy shrubs, but they seem to come to no harm from an earlier massacre.

The hellebore which queens it in January (others are still getting into training) is 'Atrorubens'. It is a deep reddish-purple sterile hybrid of uncertain parentage, although its herbaceous habit suggests *orientalis* somewhere. It could almost be called a Christmas rose, since its first blooms are expanding by then, but January is its heymonth. Its leaves are almost deciduous without actually being shed, so it is more than usually important to remove them for appearances.

Apart from occasional sorties to sniff the air, January is the month in which to find reasons (book writing is the best of them) for not being, let alone doing things, in the garden, although, of course, winter digging, draining, hedge cutting and other outdoor jobs go on, as the weather permits. The pruning of deciduous shrubs and trees most of all, as this does not depend on the ground being in any particular state; and the fact of the trees/shrubs being naked allows you to appreciate their structure and to decide where and how to thin them so as to improve their shape, let in more light and replace old branches with new.

Rose pruning can go on at any time from November to May, but it is one of those jobs I am keenest to get behind me this month. Our rose garden is enclosed by yew hedges and lies in something of a hollow, which makes it hot and airless in summer but the coldest spot in the whole garden at this time of year. But the sun shines on about half of it even at midwinter and, being a lover of creature comforts, I organize my pruning so as to be in its path between 10.00 and 3.00, when it ceases to have any power. I tackle the shady beds on dull, mild days. If some readers are shaking their heads over the idea of rose pruning in midwinter, let them leave it till later, especially if theirs is an exposed garden. I have in mind the spring rush that I know will overtake me in March (especially as I have my borders to overhaul then). Better not to have all that on my mind and rose pruning too.

Two beds containing Bourbons and hybrid perpetuals require rather more care than the rest. They make young shoots like raspberry canes and about the same length. It is a waste just to cut them hard back as though they were dwarf bushes. So, after removing last year's flowered wood, I bring all the young canes down more or less to the horizontal and fix them in that position with ash pegs *(p. 28)*. Ideal is the growth from ash stumps that were coppiced two seasons previously. In their first year they make straight rods; in their second these branch and, turned upside down, make splendid hooks. Those that are left over or still unrotted from serving the roses for one year, I also use as short pegs when layering shrubs I want to propagate this way: *Magnolia liliflora* 'Nigra' is one and *Viburnum opulus* 'Compactum' another.

The rose garden takes me about nineteen working hours to bring to orderliness and it is a quiet task with few interruptions, except by birds.

One of the nice things about gardening in winter is the birds that attend you, waiting to be fed. With the blackbirds it amounts to bullying. Even though I may not need to use a fork, I have to keep one by me to turn up worms for them. My roses are under a permanent grass mulch through which frost barely penetrates, and there are always masses of fat worms quite near the surface. When a blackbird is full to overfull, it stands hunched up with a glazed expression. No worm thrown in its direction will tempt it, in that state. But something really choice like a wireworm or beetle is more than flesh can bear. There's always a corner for morsels like that.

Left: Winter digging – John Ashbee at work – is still the best way
to deal with heavy clay soils.

Right: Ash pegs, cut from recently stooled underwood, pull the long shoots
of Bourbon and hybrid perpetual roses to the horizontal *(p. 27)*.

The lower end of the Long Border, with *Fuchsia magellanica* 'Riccartonii'
(p. 146) left and *Robinia pseudacacia* 'Rozynskiana' in the foreground.

This garden is stuffed with birds. I suppose it provides just the right cover and nesting sites for them, and a variety of habitats and food sources. The blackbirds seem most numerous of all. For the past three years or so I have had (delightful) new neighbours, bringing with them a pack of five Burmese and Siamese cats. They are compulsive hunters. When long grass is being cut, they form a circle, waiting to pounce on the mice that have been exposed.

Naturally they do not stop short at mice. Even grass snakes have been known to fall their victims, which does not please me. Neither are there many birds that I am keen to lose, though Thérèse did once catch a bullfinch and was lavishly praised for her prowess by master and mistress. She must have wondered why. Albert Croft, my very Sussex gardener who is quite a field naturalist and particularly enjoys badger watching and photography in his spare time, declared that the cats were wiping out our blackbirds.

However, there is an orchard of Bramleys and Blenheims at the top of our garden, immediately abutting our neighbours and their pets. We don't pick and store one tenth of the crop, in most years, and I leave the remainder on the ground where they fall, for the birds to make use of in due course. Up till Christmas they are disregarded. But with the first frosty spell, down come the blackbirds, thrushes (both kinds), fieldfares and redwings in their hordes, but especially the blackbirds. On one recent morning Albert counted eighty-two of them! Perhaps we shall hear less about decimation by cats for a little while.

Writing about January has one merit. I'm in the month; I don't have to imagine it. It's all around me, the wind roaring in the chimney when I'm indoors, or through the bare ash boughs that flank our western boundary when I'm out. And there's always something that it's nice to see. I like the self-sown ivies that grow up those ash trees. They take on different shapes and their greenery is cheering. It intrigues me the way my conifers – 'Ellwood's Gold' and 'Rheingold', for instance – are so much more highly coloured on their south-facing sides than the paler, greener aspect of their north-facing branches. I should hardly have expected the weak light of winter to make such a difference, and yet theirs are winter colourings, so it evidently does.

The broad-leaved evergreens in really frosty weather look utterly forlorn and dejected, their leaves hanging lustreless and limp. But the days are perceptibly lengthening and the weather is always changing, with hope just around the corner.

The best thing about January is the back of it.

February

---◆---

THINGS are looking up by February, with the days nearly two hours longer at the end of the month than they were at the start. It is the last winter month and the shortest.

There are two kinds of February. The one is a continuation of all that is nastiest about January. There is a general tendency for weather to persist to type at certain times of the year, and this is one of them. If winter had us in its grip in January, it is disinclined to loosen it. Conversely, and giving us the second face of February, if it was mild, wet Atlantic weather at the turn of the month with south-westerlies predominant, so it may well continue, and this pitches us straight into spring. Sometimes the weather plays tricks, however, and one set of signals is followed by the 'wrong' answers. No wonder we make such a hobby of our weather.

For a blanket of snow to persist all – or even half – the month is rare indeed, and it is in February that the snowdrop season reaches its peak. My mother loved to spread snowdrops around into all sorts of odd corners and hedge or shrub bottoms, where you would not, in summer, have thought that there was room for anything, but in winter, when the leaves are off, there is. She would dig up a fat snowdrop clump after it had flowered, pull the bulbs apart, and then carry them in a trug on her arm until she saw a likely spot into which to pop a few. Then on to the next, and the next.

Her habit, when you went round the garden with her, arm in arm except along what she called the bachelor paths that were too narrow for two abreast, was suddenly to freeze (like a pointer) in front of something she meant you to look at. No word was spoken; you had to look until you spotted it. In the year following a snowdrop distribution, you would see that snowdrops were flowering where no snowdrops were before.

So we have them in a good many places – I have spread them around myself – and a bunch picked and brought into the house smells like a honey pot. We only had the common unselected snowdrop, *Galanthus nivalis*, in those days, and its double form, of which we were not nearly so fond. I rather

Opposite: The Barn and Sunk Gardens on a winter's afternoon.

Galanthus nivalis 'Samuel Arnott' growing through a patch of aubrieta underneath a white Persian lilac. This snowdrop increases freely and is boldly effective.

took the view that a snowdrop is a snowdrop and that it was mere nit-picking to distinguish between different kinds when the differences were so small. But then I would be shown, perhaps offered, one that clearly had an interesting personality of its own, and then another. I have never collected them deliberately, as I haven't the collector's mentality, but I have, over the last twenty years, acquired a dozen distinct kinds and I do like them.

Margery Fish gave me three bulbs of 'Samuel Arnott' just before she died, and I think this is the finest snowdrop I have or, indeed, that I have seen. It is vigorous and easily increased and its flowers are larger than straight *nivalis*, without being in any way coarsened. The stems are longer and stronger, too, and the flowers open over quite a long period, not all within a few days. That extends a colony's total flowering season.

Of the doubles, I delight in 'Hippolyta' (Richard Nutt gave me that), although you have to turn a flower towards you before you can see the intricate neatness with which its central rosette is arranged.

The earliest of the snowflakes, *Leucojum vernum*, is at its peak this month, and although it is short-stemmed, as befits the season, its bells are of the largest and they are usually borne in pairs if you have the right strain. It grieves me that I have never succeeded with this under meadow conditions. Led on by the easy-going *L. aestivum*, which is as happy in turf as any daffodil, I have probably been bashing my head against this particular wall for too long. *L. vernum* is much happier beneath deciduous shrubs where it does not have to compete with grass. I have stocks that I am gradually spreading around in this way.

Unless the season is unduly tardy, the winter crocuses, especially *Crocus tomasinianus*, *C. aureus* and *C. chrysanthus*, are putting their best foot forward now, although their first appearance was last month. When they open wide on sunny days the bees besiege them, collecting pollen, while from the snowdrops they collect nectar.

'Snow Bunting', one of Ernest Bowles's selections from *C. chrysanthus*, is my favourite. The bloom is creamy white with dark stripes on the outer segments. It is not always perfectly shaped – a jag in one or other segment is quite frequent – but it is marvellously honey-scented and it is one of the very first of its species in flower. There are many more, in shades of yellow, bronze, cream and blue, and they all intermarry promiscuously but happily. They are concentrated in our front meadow with the other winter flowerers. The pale toothpicks of *C. tomasinianus* open out mauve and look jolly with the deep orange yellow *C. aureus*.

C. tomasinianus is a great self-seeder and it has made its way into many of our borders, being equally happy in sun or in shade. I never think of it as a weed. If it is in my way when I'm planting something else, I ignore it, although I may out of charity push any of its corms that come to the surface in summer back under with the tip of my finger.

Rabbits are fond of crocuses, and if I lose most of my bloom and the tips of the leaves, it is because they have entered the garden. In fact it is a good plan to burn up accumulated rubbish on our several heaps, at this stage, otherwise the does will make their stabs (as we call their short breeding holes, in Sussex) in them and there'll be a young generation making the garden its permanent home.

February is a great month for hellebores. If the foliage of the *orientalis* types which we call Lenten Roses is looking tatty, and it generally is, I cut it all away just before the first blooms open. My main patch is underneath some deciduous magnolias. I prefer the lighter shades. The near-black seedlings which get some of my friends so excited don't show up well until you're so close that you can see the whites of their anthers.

Under the same magnolia umbrella I have the shrubby *Helleborus lividus corsicus*, its glaucous leaves in threes and margined with mock prickles. The flowers make dense heads (almost like a hydrangea's) of pale green saucers. Also our native stinking hellebore, *H. foetidus* (don't worry; it has no stench), which is hard to beat. The dark green foliage is uncommonly handsome and I like its bell-shaped flowers, green but stained with purple around the rim. This has also sown itself into some nearby dry walling, which divides the Long Border from the orchard. The position suits it well, although I should never have thought of it for myself.

Some of the green-flowered *Clematis* species bear a close resemblance to their hellebore relatives. In a suitable year, but not every year, *C. cirrhosa balearica* can be a great feature in February. Its pale green lanterns, freckled a muted red within, are by no means startling but they have great charm. Sprays picked for the house and conditioned last well and smell deliciously of lemons. It is evergreen, with a nice leaf, but it flowers freely only following a hot summer (never in the north, therefore) and its blossom can be destroyed by untimely frosts.

I find the laurel-like aucubas among the most cheerful evergreens, but they must be given the chance to grow well. This is not by planting them around public lavatories in grimy cities. The image has stuck and 'spotted laurels' are generally reviled. Another trouble is that the usual spotted aucubas are not spotted enough, merely flecked in a desultory and half-hearted manner.

I grow *Aucuba japonica* 'Crotonifolia', under the magnolias. It is festively blotched with yellow and most cheerfully brings light into a dark situation. Sprays picked for the house last in water for months and will give substance to a long succession of arrangements. This clone happens to be a male, so by its side I planted a female called 'Longifolia', with long, slinky, plain green leaves. It is a smart shrub at all times, but it is in February that it ripens its oval berries, twice the size of a holly's, and changing from green to red. Most berries have disappeared by now, so it is good to have this crop coming along.

Skimmia japonica berries, exceptionally, are generally disregarded by the birds in my garden and will often hang on from autumn till June. This is another shrub bearing the sexes on separate plants, and the males are worth their place for their mass of scented blossom and also, thanks to selections like 'Rubella', because their clusters of flower buds take on a rich reddish glow in autumn which persists until they open to white stars in April.

Self-sown seedlings are always turning up, and I was looking at one such the other day that was covered with flower buds for the first time. No trouble to sex it. On males, which this one is, the flower buds are gathered into mounded panicles in each of which there are many more buds than the far

Clematis cirrhosa balearica flowers in the depths of winter,
and always most freely following a hot summer. Hard weather ruins the display,
but its evergreen foliage is always an asset.

discreeter females. The ratio in one that I counted was 77:18. This sort of evidence could be useful to gardeners who suspect that they have two bushes of one sex instead of one of each (for pollination purposes), but are at a loss to know which sex theirs are. Of course you can sex a plant when it is in flower if you know how to distinguish the male organs from the female, but the flowering season is short, whereas the evidence from buds is present for six or seven months and requires little expertise to decode.

Wall peaches will be in bloom any time from the beginning of next month and they need a copper spray before that – two sprayings, in fact, at three-week intervals – to protect their young foliage against the fungus causing peach leaf curl. Those bloated pustules are most unpleasant to see, and affected leaves, which will be the majority in a bad year, drop off, seriously weakening the plant. We also treat the dwarf almond, *Prunus tenella*, which is subject to the same ailment as are tree almonds, but I don't grow any of them as they make ungainly specimens and have nothing to offer after March. Apricots, of which we have one large tree – and that will be flowering even before the peaches – fortunately don't suffer from leaf curl. But while there's copper in the can we spray those of our daphnes that are susceptible to anthracnose, a killer defoliating fungus disease caused by *Marssonina daphnes*; this treatment, repeated whenever we're using copper (for instance against blight of tomatoes and potatoes later on), has been effective. *Daphne mezereum*, *D. odora* and *D. pontica* are among the most susceptible, while *D. tangutica* and *D. retusa* have never been troubled.

But to return to my peaches. It is obviously more thrifty to prune them before spraying than after, and anyway peaches grow against warm walls so that, with sun on your back and an interesting problem in front of you, it is a pleasant occupation. The aim is to remove all of last year's fruited wood and to tie in young shoots for flowering and fruiting this year. Ideally these will be straight rods about 18 inches long. Too short, and they'll be too weak; cut these out. Too strong and watery and they'll probably be difficult to tie in at all and in any case will not fruit. Such branches occur most frequently on young trees, and some of them can be used to build up the framework of a plant not yet covering the area allotted to it. The golden rule when tying in is never to let any branch cross over any other. The top dog will shade its victim, which cannot prosper.

Morello cherries are pruned at the same time and in the same way, but as they're grown against north walls, the task is less popular! The apricot is pruned just before it flowers, too, but this mainly buds up from spurs off the older wood, so it's a question, here, of cutting out the weak and tying in all that won't be overcrowded of the rest. Our apricot is older than I am and therefore quite a veteran. It ripens the most luscious fruit, in August, but only if the blackbirds leave it alone. There's no practical method of protection.

The wall figs need sorting over in February, too. These are the variety 'Brunswick' and they were planted for their ornamental foliage, which is handsomely indented. However, I have a passion for green figs (and my mother before me). 'Brunswick' is the largest fruited that we can ripen outside, but it crops irregularly, generally every third or fourth year. The less you prune a fig the better, from the cropping angle, as this year's figs are currently present as tiny pimples near the tips of last year's new shoots. So you leave as many of these as you can. A major thinning and retraining is generally necessary every third year, otherwise the fig will no longer be the wall specimen intended. In some places this wouldn't matter. Then you can let it become a tree.

A winter job that we complete in February, if not before, is the mulching of young trees planted in turf. Most of them are in the orchard, but I must explain that I never, nowadays, plant an orchard fruit tree because the bird damage to flower buds is more than I am prepared to cope with. And yet there isn't much room for trees at Dixter, except in the orchard or other meadow areas. Where there are yew hedges, as in most of the rest of the garden, trees would not be appropriate. So I plant, instead of fruit, such trees as I want to grow and that will not become ridiculously large. (My mother said I was making a botanical garden of the place and she had a point.) Most of them, like *Sorbus* and *Crataegus*, belong to the *Rosaceae*, and some of them are stripped by bullfinches in some years – *Crataegus prunifolia*, for instance.

A young tree planted in turf is in a terribly competitive situation from the grass, both for water and nutrients. The grass itself is composted, and we use this compost as a generous mulch around young trees for their first five years or however long it seems to be taking them to become thoroughly established. But we first remove encroaching couch and other grasses and cow parsley from around them, and after the mulch has gone on and settled, we water it with a pre-emergence weedkiller (Lenacil), which puts paid to competition from annual weeds, apart from *Veronica hederifolia*, the ivy speedwell, which is resistant.

We also clean out under the yew hedges, to make sure that ivy seedlings cannot take over here. And we weed the gap kept between a hedge and turf (mown or rough), again following up with weedkiller. Then the hedges are given a feed of organic fertilizer: meat, blood and bone – it makes them sound like ravening monsters.

Actually they do look handsome at this time of year when the garden's bareness reveals them without distractions. And I have to confess that their clipping is not completed, nowadays, until February (although every year we hope we shall do better). Ideally, you clip in August (and only once a year, thank heavens; none of that 'Can we get away with doing it twice or must we clip them a third time?' that you have with Leyland cypress), which is late enough not to be followed by a further flush of growth. The yews will then retain their sharp, shaven outlines right through till the end of May. Only then does a fuzz of new shoots start to blur their profile.

In the old days, five or six men set about them with shears and the task was soon completed. But now, even with a mechanized trimmer, there seem to be so many distractions.

The pussies of *Salix daphnoides* 'Aglaia' are prominent from January onwards, while the young stems are tinged red – a small tree that looks agreeable at every season.

All the yews were planted by my father except the one numbered 8 on the plan at the beginning of the book *(p. 6)*, a little off the south-east end of the house. This was a free-growing tree which my father cut back, leaving only its trunk and some branch stumps, then trained into a tiered conical specimen. It stands at the brink of that rough grass hollow (where once the house sewage seeped) which I mentioned in my Introduction *(p. 16)*. In this I have a willow, *Salix daphnoides* 'Aglaia', whose large silver pussies are prominent now, especially seen against the yew's dark bulk. It makes quite a sizeable tree, but for the sake of catkin production (biggest is best being my motto, in this instance) I cut it pretty hard back from time to time. When it takes umbrage and begins to die in patches, there is nothing easier than to start a new one (and get rid of the old). I take a thick stem about 3 or 4 ft long and a couple of inches across, and push it as far as I can into the soft, squelchy ground. It becomes a new tree forthwith.

I love this willow at every season. You notice its reddish-purple stems in winter. Many of them grow horizontally and are often hung with rows of pearly raindrops, catching the light. In summer its foliage is elegant, never heavy like oak and beech.

Although the wild ivy berries are still green, they are just at that stage when the woodpigeons have an insatiable desire to eat them. The pigeon is a heavy (and what a handsome) bird and not self-evidently designed by its Maker to perch at the extremity of ivy twigs and reach out for berries. So there is a terrible clattering of wings as a pair of garden habitués balance precariously and at the same time make a desperate lunge for the coveted morsels. The noise is deafening; who said the countryside was peaceful?

The Horse Pond *(p. 41)* looks clean and open, the water itself at its clearest; no weed obstruction, no murky algae, while waterlily leaves are in abeyance. There are willows fringing the drive-side bank, but they are pollarded to low stools every other year. There is usually some occasion, each winter, when ice is thick enough to walk on, but whenever the water is ice-free (more than half the time) and not too much ruffled by wind (but even then the catspaws are fun to watch), the carmine stems of dogwood, *Cornus alba*, on the far bank are reflected and glow if there's any sun to touch them. This is just about my favourite part of the garden.

Provided you do not try to maintain beds of marginal plants like primulas and astilbes, which are hell to keep weed-free, as every weed pulled brings with it a pound or two of soggy soil, I reckon that water gardening is low on maintenance demands. One weeding a year, by someone who is prepared to get into the water and pull such weeds as *Glyceria maxima* or *Typha latifolia*, is all that's necessary.

But for some eight recent years we were plagued by one of those aggressive underwater oxygenators, *Elodea crispa*, with trails of growth like spring coils, which took over the entire pond, apart from the waterlilies, and even these were being hemmed in and reduced. You no longer saw any water at all. A moorhen could walk over the surface, and flag irises were seeding into and germinating in the weed. Unfortunately the public seem to feel that a pond is anyone's property, and we have actually seen individuals bringing tadpoles or fish, surplus to their requirement, along and tipping them into our pond. With them there'll be water and weeds, so it is easy enough for a scourge like this to make its entry unrecorded.

A long and costly battle, first by pulling, which proved to be futile, then with dire weedkillers (Diquat, marketed as Reglone), at last got rid of the weed – and of many precious plants, but not of the waterlilies themselves, which are tough as blazes, nor of the countless fish. Before the elodea, there was water violet, *Hottonia palustris* (it grows wild in the Rother marshes below us), as the main underwater oxygenator and it was entirely satisfactory. You need one or other of these, otherwise the water will be taken over by hideous algae, such as blanket weed, and it will always be turbid. Hottonia in winter makes great green cloud banks of finely divided foliage arranged in rosettes, while in May it flowers delightfully, rather like candelabras of pale mauve *Primula malacoides*, to which it is related – not to violets. After the holocaust, we re-introduced a few seedlings from a dyke on the marsh and they took.

We were not out of the nightmare yet, however. *Elodea canadensis*, which is only slightly less ferocious than *E. crispa*, had somehow got in and that spread like wildfire. So it was back to the poison gun. As far as I can see, at the time of writing, we are clear again and there's still quite a bit of water violet surviving. You cannot live without hope, so it pays to be optimistic.

I count vegetables from the garden among life's major pleasures, and winter vegetables are no less enjoyable in their way than those of summer. But as this is primarily a flower garden (not forgetting foliage), vegetables are not always given attention at just that moment when it is needed. And so in every year there are failures and disappointments, but in every year, also, there are compensating successes.

I like to grow some waxy maincrop potatoes, because these are not generally popular in Britain and you never find them in the shops. 'Pink Fir Apple' is a favourite, not just for salads but also for boiling and eating hot. The tubers take on extraordinary shapes but, by way of compensation, they're easy to peel after cooking – until the end of the season when (by April) they mysteriously become difficult. Shallots are the only other vegetable I eat from store, not growing onions which are easily bought at any season.

Carrots are infinitely better flavoured straight from the ground, even accepting the damage that small black subterranean slugs will do them there. Neither do I store celeriac, of which I grow a lot because it is just as tasty as celery but much less trouble to grow well, given a heavy slug-infested soil like ours. Celeriac will be spoilt by heavy frosts, but I reckon to be eating it from late October onwards, so that if it catches it in February, most of the crop will already have been eaten. Often, though, I can eat it to the last root, in April.

The Horse Pond in winter.

This is a vegetable I never tire of, whereas parsnips, delicious though they are with a roast, are not for every day. Neither are Jerusalem artichokes. With all the flatulence they engender, five or six dishes in a winter are enough. Scorzonera and salsify (also Composites) have the same gastric effect, but I always grow one or other or even both of these. Though it needs the more cooking, I do believe salsify has the more pronounced flavour.

Leeks are the greatest standby and never stale. I don't reckon to weigh into leeks before December but they'll usually serve me into April, by which time their stems develop a hard core which is the flower stalk. Beet is sometimes frosted in the winter garden; its roots are terribly exposed.

Brussels sprouts are the most important brassica. I grow a mid-season and a late variety, but also draw heavily upon the sprouting sprouts for spring greens later on. I like a row of 'January King' cabbages, too; they are

February weather is often mild; grey *Helichrysum splendidum*
contrasts with *Chamaecyparis thyoides* 'Ericoides' behind it on 'conifer corner'.
The laurustinus was bird-sown from our neighbour's colony.

excellently flavoured. Purple sprouting broccoli is a choice but dicy crop, taking nearly a year to grow and often set upon by our all too tame pigeons in late winter or early spring. This seems not to be an important crop to processors for freezing, and there are therefore no F1 strains and the open-pollinated ones are all extremely variable in their performance. In a way this is quite convenient, because you get a good spread of cropping period as between plants. I always buy seed of the so-called 'Early Purple Sprouting', and although most of it waits till April, I'm pleased if some, in some years, will crop in February.

I think salads are almost as important in winter as in summer. I take the view that lettuce should be given a rest from November to April or May, and why not? There are plenty of alternatives. Winter glasshouse lettuces are fragile, tasteless and expensive, though I must confess to being tempted by the recent influx of foreign iceberg lettuces, which are really solid and do have flavour.

But of my own growing I'm happy with chicory. The Witloof kind is in my cellar, or on the slightly warmer stairs leading down to it. It is cropping now. So, if we grow them well, are the green sugarloaf chicories from the garden. Their outer leaves are soon frosted, so that they look pretty terrible, but when these are peeled off, the dense, bullet-shaped hearts are still in perfect order. There are several variously marked and coloured, non-hearting leaf chicories in the Saladisi seed mixture that we sowed in early July, and these are making tasty new leaves now. I also grow corn salad in some years, sown in September, and the delicious young shoots of chives are already pickable. I only have the giant kind, which is showy in flower and just as good to eat as the traditional smaller kind with miserable little flowers.

On average, February is one of our drier months (partly because it is also shorter), sometimes the driest of the year. I always have the hope that it will produce some weather allowing me, for the first time since early November, to stretch out on my back on a south-facing bank in our orchard (overlooking the rubbish heap), after lunch, and bask in the sun. If I bring a rug with me Tulipa, my dachshund, will share it. If not, she sits firmly on my stomach, which is a good vantage point until she sees something to chase, whereupon I am used as a springboard, but at least I have all the sun to myself again.

One pleasure is certain. I shall hear the blackbirds singing for the first time since early last July. There'll be others joining in: chaffinches, blue and great tits for instance, but the blackbird's liquid notes are my favourite bird song, and never mind that they're only swearing at one another. Interpretation can be left to others. The sound is enough for me.

March

———◆———

L IKE farmers and fishermen, gardeners are close to the weather. In a state of continual tizz that it will do what they hope yet without transgressing the bounds of what seems 'right' for the season, they become superstitious. It only requires an unseasonably mild day or two any time between October and April and they'll be shaking their heads on the dismal 'We'll pay for it later' principle. The idea of retribution dies hard. Wouldn't you rather have good weather now and pay for it later than, quite possibly, not have it at all? I believe in seizing the moment and in taking what follows as it comes.

Give me a fine March day with the sound of flies and bees in the air and I'm on top of the world. So are you, but don't let it rush to your head by sowing every packet of seed in your pile without stopping to think how you'll keep all those seedlings happy when they need more space or when colder weather returns. It's one thing to have a propagator in which you can germinate the seeds of half hardy annuals at the optimum temperature, but what's to be their fate after that? They'll need pricking out, which will occupy ten times as much space. Have you room to keep them warm and growing without a check? If so, you're wealthy. The ground will not be warm enough to plant these half-hardies out with profit to them until the end of May at the earliest. Two to three months is a long time to keep them happy without signs of overcrowding or starvation.

I sow only a few seeds in March: some lettuce 'Little Gem', in a pot; a box of old-fashioned, extra-sweet-scented sweet peas, space sown; plain-leaved parsley, which is the most aromatic – just a few things that are pretty hardy and need a long growing season. The only heat they get is from the sun.

I should explain that for all my propagations I use home-made double-walled, double glass-glazed cold frames. They have 2-inch concrete walls, inside and out, with an insulating space between. The inner lights are horizontal, thus retaining and returning most of the moisture that condenses on them. The outer lights slope, to throw the rain off. This double glazing

Opposite: *Alnus cordata* grows near the Lower Moat.
It is the latest alder in flower and carries the boldest catkins.

retains much accumulated day warmth far into the night, but if nights are cold we additionally cover them with one of our strips of hessian. I have been doing this for over thirty years now and find it both cheap and effective.

Nothing is sown in the open ground until the end of April, as our clay soil long remains cold and often wet and is not easily worked to a seed-bed-fine tilth. I make no direct sowings of annuals in the borders, either. If it's dry, the sparrows will indulge in dust baths, if wet and then dry, the soil pans and cracks. Weed seeds germinate and grow faster than the annuals one has sown, so that competition is immediately fierce. I find that annuals of all kinds, hardy or not, get away to a far more propitious start if brought on under glass initially and then planted out when already a good size, though not drawn or crowded, if I can help it.

March is the first spring month. Statistics tell us, and I can believe them, that we can expect more snow now than in December, but however vile the weather, there is a great surge of activity in the animal and vegetable world.

A deafening (unless you're already deaf) dawn chorus develops, as the month proceeds. The birds are gathering absurdly large beakfuls of nesting material. The first and easiest nests to spot are the mistle thrush's. Shy though this bird is, it plonks them in thoroughly exposed places like the crutch of our William's pear tree. These early efforts rarely meet with success. There are plenty of magpies on the watch for eggs and nestlings, and I can't help admiring these handsome, crafty birds. They have to earn a living after their own fashion, and think what a hopeless population explosion and consequent famine there would be in the bird world if there were no predators to keep things under control. It's bad enough to have killed off our falcons, kites and vultures.

The most poignant domestic signal of spring's return to Great Dixter is the mating call of the death watch beetle as it taps its head against a reverberating surface. Woodpeckers, go home.

The screws are on this month to have the garden tidy in readiness for opening our gates to the public on 1 April (or even earlier if Easter falls in March). We never entirely give up mowing the lawns during the winter, but they'll need another cut and edging. Most important of all, the Long Border – seventy yards long and fifteen feet deep in its main part – must be overhauled. The days are as long as one could wish them, by now, and with cooperation from the weather, two of us getting at it without excess interruption can have it done in six days. The remains of herbaceous perennials like phlox, aconitum and miscanthus are paper light and very easily removed. The first two don't even need cutting down. They break off at ground level. A lot of oak leaves will always have drifted into the front of the border from the slip of woodland below the orchard. They'll need rounding up. There'll be some shrubs, like buddleias, penstemons, fuchsias and santolina, to prune; others I may already have dealt with. Groups of perennials will need splitting and replanting in improved soil.

The improving material is deep litter chicken manure, the litter being sawdust. This is light and clean to handle, rich in nutrients but weed-free; worth keeping chickens for, in fact. The whole border gets a dressing, and soon after that's on I go round all the borders and the raspberry cage with Growmore pellets as a boost at the start of a new growing season. The cage area has previously been heavily mulched with half-decayed garden compost. Another little job in the cage that I usually have to catch up with now is pruning the gooseberries and the currants, black and red.

One good point about leaving border work until spring is that you don't inadvertently harm or dig up your permanently resident tulip population. Most of these are nestled near to deciduous shrubs like summer tamarisk or hydrangeas, or among perennials like Japanese anemones that seldom need upheaving. The tulips are all well through, and you only have to take care not to step back on them with a heedless heel.

Hydrangeas, of which I like every kind, receive maximum attention in March. I want them constantly to renew themselves from the inside of the bush and I want to prevent their overall circumference from becoming too bulky. So, with my saw and secateurs, my kneeling board and kneeling mat, I crawl under and into them and sort out all the oldest branches. No wood in the hortensia and lacecap hydrangeas will be more than four years old. There is total renewal, but it is spread as evenly as possible over the years. After their pruning, they also receive a chicken manure and Growmore dressing. This is the time to encourage their greed, not in summer or early autumn when late growth would be too soft to survive the winter.

I forgot to mention their dead heads, but these scarcely require separate treatment from the branches that are anyway being removed and on which most of the flowers were located.

New hydrangea leaves and shoots have a stimulatingly sharp smell. March is not a leafy month, so the unfolding of new leaves is especially noticeable. On elders these are dark and sullen, but very fresh dotted all over the hawthorns and quick hedges. *Sorbus meliosmifolia* is one of my earliest trees in leaf, bronzed when young, and this is good to bring indoors; its clusters of cream blossom are already expanding in April. It's an uncommon beam with plain oval leaves like a hornbeam.

Colchicum foliage first showed through in January but now expands, rich and glossy. Sure, it is voluminous but that's no excuse for the fuss against colchicums that you too often hear in respect of their foliage. As it begins to yellow and before it collapses over neighbouring plants in May–June, you have merely to cut it away. That's in the borders. In rough grass, of course, the grass itself overtakes the colchicums and you don't notice their exit.

Crown imperials, *Fritillaria imperialis*, are no less lush and they draw attention to themselves by the terrific pong, half fox, half garlic, that floats around them. By the time their shoots are 6 or 9 inches tall you can see whether they have buds in them or whether, as is so often my fate, they are blind. I've never made this bulb really happy and evidence of how to please it conflicts wildly.

Foliage that encroaches nearer on my appetites is the new growth on tarragon, new leaves on sorrel, *Rumex scutatus*, wherewith to make soups, and the lushest growth of the year, without too much flower and seed, on the hairy bitter cress, *Cardamine hirsuta*. This is a weed which we are busy eliminating (as far as we ever can) in March, but its flavour is good and it makes a welcome ingredient in salads. So, at the last moment, after the salad has been dressed, do the flowers of violets and primroses.

Sweet-scented violets are the first of their kind to flower and they grow all over the garden, their favourite haunts and where they least need to be disturbed being under deciduous trees and shrubs and in certain paving cracks that get missed by weedkiller, to which, in any case, they are strongly resistant. There is also an area beneath shrub roses that we regularly treat with simazine, and the violets are prominent here. Their great scourge is the violet leaf midge, which puffs their leaves up into bloated bolsters. It is both unsightly and weakening and there is, in the circumstances, no practical remedy. Our violets are many-hued – pink, white, apricot, violet and mauve. My mother loved to collect them and was especially proud of the bright pink ones. We have most of the white, and I think that is my favourite.

Celandines, *Ranunculus ficaria*, come into their own in March and I have several of the garden forms, of which the neat buttons of the double yellow, green-centred kind is one of the prettier. My special pride is 'Brazen Hussy', a clone I put up to the R.H.S. and which received an Award of Merit. From time to time (mine is not, I understand, the only recorded instance) celandines sport to a purple-leaved clone against which their yellow flowers show up dramatically. Mine occurs as quite a patch in Four Acre Shaw, which is a small wood about a quarter of a mile from Dixter, and that is where I spotted it.

Two celandines, *Ranunculus ficaria,* filling the gap between lawn and yew hedge.
The green-eyed double is an old-fashioned flower. The other, 'Brazen Hussy', with
purple foliage, I found as a sport growing wild in a nearby wood.

Wood anemones belong to March, too, and we have lots of them in the
garden, mostly introduced unintentionally. They cope well with rough grass
and look comfortable there, opening wide stars to the sun. All the native
windflowers in this part of the country are white, with a pink flush
developing on the outside as the flower ages. But in Ireland there is a greater
range of colour and I am particularly fond of a late-flowering blue clone from
Lismore, on the borders of Counties Cork and Waterford, given me by my
Dutch friend, Romke, when he was working there. It has established beneath
birch trees near the Horse Pond.

In this ill-drained area, largely colonized by two species of rush, I have had
great success with *Narcissus minor*, which is a yellow trumpet daffodil and like
a miniature version of our native Lent lily, *Narcissus pseudonarcissus. N. minor*
was given me from a North Irish garden, twenty years ago. If you want to
work up stocks quickly, the best way is to plant bulbs singly in a border.
When they have clumped up well, lift and split them and plant all but one
(which is returned to its original position to start the good work again) in

Narcissus 'Tête-à-Tête' is a vigorous and early flowering mini-trumpet daffodil,
here flowering in the High Garden.

rough grass. Increase will be much slower, here, but it has been cumulative
and this tiny daffodil looks just right in its unpretentious context.

Of the Lent lily itself, also reaching its peak in March, our main concentration is in the meadow areas just inside the front gate. Their freedom of
flowering fluctuates noticeably from year to year, but there can be no doubt
about their feeling at home. They seed themselves generously.

'Tête-à-tête' looks like a first cousin to the last two species, but the fact of
having two blooms back to back on some of its stems earns this name.

In the orchard, on the other side of the house, the daffodils are still only
coming on but you can see, by looking down on the clumps, how freely they
are budded and what kind of show they will shortly be making. In the
meantime there will, rabbits permitting, be a fine show of Dutch crocuses.

The yellows, which form clumps, are first in flower. The mauves, whites, purples and stripies, of which there is also a carpet in the Upper Moat, overlap and follow. As these are self-seeders, you are not so much aware of them in clusters as in a more or less dense scatter. They are mainly concentrated outside the daffodil areas, but have worked their way into these, too, and show up well wherever they are because the daffodils are still short enough not to conceal them. Much as I love daffodils, I unquestionably lean towards the crocuses because of the spontaneous way they open to sunshine, which echoes my own expansive feelings from the same cause.

Tulips have this gladdening habit too, and the first of these, derivatives of *Tulipa kaufmanniana*, will be out before the end of the month. But they do not prosper and increase with us like the later tulips. And I have never really succeeded with tulips over a long period in a meadow setting. The competition seems to be too much for them. And yet I still feel that, given the right tulip, probably a species, it should be on. Perhaps with a free-flowering strain of the scented, yellow *T. sylvestris*. Too often this is barren, probably because our summers are not hot enough to ripen the bulbs.

It seems odd to write of tulips and snowdrops as contemporaries, but there is an overlap at either end of their seasons. Snowdrops (discounting the autumn-flowering *Galanthus nivalis reginae-olgae*) start soon after Christmas, and tulips end in June with *T. sprengeri*. *Galanthus platyphyllus* is usually at its best in mid-March, but often, in the shady place I have it (you need take no notice of those who tell you it *prefers* sun), flowers into April. Its synonym is *G. ikariae latifolius*. In its native Caucasus it flowers in May–June near the snow line.

This is a happy species that multiplies readily by self-seeding – always the most satisfactory way of naturalizing. Its broad leaves are not in the least glaucous, like most snowdrops, but are bright bay green and glossy. The flowers have rather pointed outer segments which lend it a come-hitherish expression. It will seed into paving cracks.

Two scillas – *Scilla sibirica* and *S. bithynica* – are fairly notable at Dixter, although I also have *S. bifolia* and *S. verna* (from wild seed). *S. sibirica* is the brightest, bluest and largest-flowered ('Spring Beauty' is identical) and everyone's favourite. Taking my cue from Hidcote, although I have not been there to see them at the right time, I have interplanted a bed of fuchsias with them and they actually thrive a lot better than the fuchsias in a badly drained spot that receives far too much rainwater (thanks to a defective gutter) off a very expansive roof. We're doing something about the drainage as I write, but it's interesting that the scillas are undeterred. They make a marvellous splash, but you need to cut the dead-looking fuchsia wood back before this starts. I've tried them over and again in rough grass, but they won't take it for many years.

S. bithynica is a strong grower and inclined to the takeover bid. There were sheets of it in Collingwood Ingram's Benenden garden, about nine miles from me, and he gave it to many visitors. It is a self-seeding carpeter and ideal beneath deciduous shrubs and trees which will later make such a dense cover that nothing can be seen or will grow beneath them. The colour varies from a weak skimmed-milk off-white through to a decent shade of blue, though never intense like *sibirica*. Cherry (as he was known) used to try to improve the strain by weeding out all the pale, washy specimens, but I doubt if he ever made much headway. Surprising how little this obliging species is offered; not at all by the big houses.

A Dutch botanist friend who is also a splendid illustrator was staying with me one spring and I asked him to decorate the top of a pie I had made with the surplus pastry. He'd done a lively scene of dachshunds among rushes on a previous occasion, but this time he chose to do a beautiful little group of the dog's tooth violet, *Erythronium dens-canis*. A shame it couldn't be preserved.

The reappearance of this flower is the most exciting of the month's events, I do believe. Only a week or so elapses between its first pushing through of purple snouts to the opening, mid-month, of its flowers. They are pinky-mauve turkscaps, which open out by day but close to rest, and they are surrounded by their miraculously marbled foliage in pale green and maroon.

Scilla bithynica fills in nicely under a deciduous shrub like this magnolia, beneath which it will later be too dark for anything to grow.

Narcissus minor and *Erythronium dens-canis* make a pretty pair, but I photographed them rather too early in the morning, before the dog's-tooth violet had reflexed its petals. The mulch of oak leaves is for the nearby rhododendrons.

They do not seed with me. I should make a point of introducing another clone for the sake of pollination. But they clump up and I divide them after flowering. No need to grow them in a border. They increase well in rather thin turf such as you find beneath a tree or on a cool, north-facing bank.

On such a bank, and also by the Horse Pond and, again, in the Long Border, I grow the south-west European toothwort, *Lathraea clandestina*. It is a parasite on tree roots, and is best known on willow but also on poplar and maple. In fact I don't think it's very particular.

How to establish a parasite? Seed pushed into the soil close to a likely tree root is one method (though a slow one), and seed is on offer. I was given a lump of lathraea roots in soil and I planted them in three different places, all near willows. That was in the autumn, and there was great excitement, eighteen months later, when the first dense clusters of bright purple, hooded flowers appeared, close to ground level. They liven up the Long Border at a dead season near to *Salix alba* 'Argentea', which I grow for its silvery foliage contrasting in summer with the yellow of 'Dickson's Golden' elm. But the parasite has spread quite a way along the yew hedge bottom at the back of the border, and I suspect it has taken on a new host. So also on the cool north-facing bank at the bottom of which I started it on a rather weakly goat willow, *Salix caprea*. The willow is weaker still now, but the lathraea goes from strength to strength and is travelling among some rhododendrons. Do try and grow this one. It adds something extra to your garden without any demands on space. From a distance it looks like clumps of crocuses but its season is far longer.

Many of my horticultural friends are horrified by abnormalities, even if they have nothing diseased about them (John Bond looks as though a bad smell had been put under his nose when he sees, for instance, a disorganized variegation). And so I doubt whether *Salix sachalinensis* 'Sekka' will ever win an Award of Merit from the R.H.S., however often and however beautifully it is presented. Many of its branches, if you keep it regularly pruned, are flattened in one plane and broadened in the opposite. They twist into beautiful scrolls. Added to the fact that the young bark is a bright glossy brown, male catkins (for this is a male clone) covered with yellow pollen are borne abundantly in late March and especially on the fasciated branches.

This is a vigorous, wide-spreading shrub that requires plenty of space. Pollarded every year, it tends to go down to silver leaf disease which is a killer, so I cut mine back every two or three years and expect to have to replace it now and again. I'm very fond of it in summer and autumn, too (the leaves hang on till December), because its lance leaves are glossy and their downward curving arc catches the light on the upper surface. This is particularly lively as I drive homewards in the latter part of the day when the sun is shining from the opposite direction.

I delay pruning till the very end of the month, when flowering is over. All the palm or pussy willow, *Salix caprea*, is flowering this month at different times on different trees, and it is a great source of pollen for bees feeding their early broods. First butterflies are on the wing, too. Sometimes I'll see a Comma on *Daphne mezereum*. Peacocks and Tortoiseshells are frequent on aubrieta, and they even visit crocuses and hyacinths.

The fact that hyacinths can be so easily forced but also flowered at their natural time in the garden means that they have a four-months-long season. That suits me. Like any sensible gardener, I eventually, having had them for perhaps two or three seasons in bowls in the house, plant them out. There, if they can be left undisturbed, they will last indefinitely. An old clump of 'L'Innocence', originally given to my brother in hospital when he had appendicitis in 1929, has gone on untiringly ever since. A white like this contrasts prettily with yellow clumps of *Narcissus minor* or 'Tête-à-tête', while pink and blue hyacinths make a great showing among the young carmine stems of peony shoots – meaning the lactiflora hybrids. But I don't grow many of these, now, except for picking. As border plants their season is too short, while peony botrytis disease makes it too uncertain.

Quite a few shrubs are performing now, although in a garden so often populated by bullfinches (one pair is more than enough) it is little use my attempting blossom which they will devour. *Daphne mezereum* reaches its high point in March, and so does the anaemic *D. odora* 'Aureomarginata', which persists in holding me at arm's length. All stock is infected with virus, and as it never sets seed in cultivation we can only hope that the micro-propagators will turn their attention sooner or later to this commercially unimportant plant, and breed stock that is virus-free. It could be done.

Rhododendron nuts would not reckon me as one of their number, but there are many I'm fond of on my own terms. They are scattered over the garden – about fifty different kinds, but you'd never guess it. *Rhododendron dauricum* flowered in January; 'Tessa' and *R. × praecox* last month. Now it is the turn of *R. praevernum*, which is pale mauve with a deep purple blotch on a heavy shrub with the characteristic vices of many popular hybrids; in particular a long, leathery, lustreless leaf. But, bless it, it flowers both early, now, that is, and late. It nearly always produces some autumn clusters. I'm grateful, and anyway Cherry Ingram gave it to me as a layer from his garden. It was flowering on his hundredth birthday in October 1980 and I wrote to him about it. Spring in autumn seemed to characterize him as well as his plant so aptly.

March is a blustery month, so it is small wonder that many trees and shrubs depending on wind pollination are flowering now. There are the yews. Pollen will blow off a male yew like smoke billowing from a bonfire. We only have hedges, but it amuses me to give them a pat and see the pollen fly. My Italian cypress, *Cupressus sempervirens*, which I grew from seed collected in the Apennines in September 1956, flowers in the same way and at the same time.

Best by far are the beautiful yellow catkins on the Italian alder, *Alnus cordata (p. 44)*. They are unusually long (four inches), thick and showy. All through the winter they are held at various angles, like closed fingers pointing, mostly, to the horizontal. As they expand, they hang, and the plump female 'cones' make an appropriate contrast; this year's are green, last year's black. Alders are much underrated trees. Their more glamorous cousins, the birches, take the limelight.

April

◆

BY April, an anticyclone will be firmly established in the North Atlantic, a little south of Greenland, and will send us a series of bitterly cold fronts moving down its east flank. 'Two inches of snow overnight; very pretty,' I wrote in a recent diary on 3 April, which happened also to be Easter Day. A plague on the church calendar for pegging Easter to the phases of the moon. What holiday visitor wants to see gardens in weather so predictably like this? Only the desperate.

We are open to the public and there is nothing to show them; no big display until the maincrop daffodils are out. That'll be mid-month. Experience confirms that 16 April is a safe date on which to be sure of seeing them. They can neither be so early as to be fading by then, apart from 'Princeps', which is as early as the Lent lilies and like a polyploid version; nor so late that the maincrop 'Emperor' can fail to be performing. That is a yellow trumpet of which we have three blocks separated by three of white narcissus – a mixture of the similar 'Minnie Hume' and 'Mrs Langtry'. It was wise to alternate the yellows and the whites, the trumpets and the small cups; and it was wise to plant each area with only one variety. Mixtures always sound jolly, and as they are usually the cheapest obtainable – advertised as mixtures for naturalizing – they are difficult to resist. The idea of something of everything; what could be more delightful? In fact, as also in bedding out, mixtures merely look confused when you stand back from them. Some plants will be out and over long before others. They are an unsatisfactory mish-mash.

Besides the yellow trumpets and the white narcissi, there are three areas devoted to 'Barrii Conspicuus' (named after the once famous bulb firm of Barr). This is a yellow narcissus with a bright rim to its small cup. It is rather later flowering than the others, but the best thing about it is its warm scent which is carried on the air. There is one spot near the centre of our daffodil orchard where it has always seemed to me that there is less wind and that the sun is warmer, the atmosphere generally kinder in a private sort of way than

Opposite: In the orchard, with *Narcissus* 'Barrii Conspicuus'; 'Emperor' daffodils behind. Protective oaks form a slip of woodland beyond the Lower Moat (*pp. 75–6*).

anywhere else. A path goes through it, and my mind will be miles away when I'm approaching but suddenly I'll have this curious awareness. Could a couple have been particularly happy in this spot at some time in the past, I ask myself, and have passed on an aura of content? I don't know that anyone else has noticed it, so it's probably all in my imagination. Indeed, I had no idea of writing about it until I suddenly was.

The orchard has many moods. After a frosty night, all the daffodils are flat on their faces and their foliage too, if leaves have faces. 'That's torn it,' you think, because they look as though they'll never recover, but they do. However, if wind and rain beat them flat there's no redress. Actually, by the time the daffodil season is at an end I'm quite glad to see the grass growing through and over them. We're ready to move on to other things.

I do think, though, that this is the only way to grow the larger, taller daffodils that doesn't change them into an insufferable affliction when decay sets in. Anywhere else they stick out with horrible obtrusion, so that your garden displays an advanced state of senility before May is well begun.

As children, my mother paid us a penny a hundred to pick the dead daffodils and carry them to the rubbish heap. It would have been quicker and more sensible but less moral (and no one ever suggested it) merely to pick off the dead heads and leave the green stems to help build up the bulbs. Since we've stopped picking the deads altogether, and that long since, some interesting self-sown hybrids have turned up.

April is the busiest month of the year at Dixter. Not only have we our own work to do but we are supplying plants both to personal visitors and to mail-order customers. In the frameyard, which is our workshop, pot-grown plants that have been overwintered under glass are stood in the open again to make room for the great explosion of newly potted material from cuttings that were struck last summer and autumn.

It is a sound rule to pot off no more rooted cuttings after the end of August. The only exceptions are those plants which can continue to grow at low temperatures throughout the winter. Those that stand still will be more harmed than helped by disturbing them when they cannot make good use of their extra space and new potting soil. That this should be so is a great convenience. It means that your rooted cuttings can be overwintered 10, 12, 14 to a 3½-inch pot, the pot they were struck in, and this is extremely economical of space. By April, they can wait no longer. Space must be found, but cold glass is protection enough by then.

We start with the hydrangeas, potting those that look vigorous (and if you started with vigorous cutting material, they will be that) straight into 5-inch pots. The rest, such as fuchsias, gazanias, felicias, osteospermums, *Convolvulus mauritanicus*, *C. cneorum*, *Erysimum* 'Bowles's Mauve' and diascias, go into 3½-inch pots and John Innes No. 2 potting compost. Shrubs like cistus, ceanothus, buddleias, etc., go into the same mix and pots for a start, but will be moved into 5-inch pots and John Innes No. 3 later on. All our composts are soil-based. Loam is handy; we skim turf from a nearby field.

My own special task is to sow 80–100 packets of seed in pots and boxes, which I aim to do in the second week, leaving some (the more tender) for the end of the month, others for May and even June, where seedlings are required to follow a biennial like sweet williams.

There is a lot of planting and moving to get on with in the garden. If you don't leave things out of the ground for any length of time, plants can go on being moved right into summer. Naturally we keep a hose handy.

April is the ideal month for making a new artichoke bed. Ideally I'd like a new one every year, scrapping the old bed after its second season. In practice I often have to leave a bed down for three years. The two-year system works so well because your second-year bed will crop from late May till July, while your new bed will take over from July and carry on till autumn. As I and my friends eat a great many artichokes and never tire of them, this is a splendid arrangement. The beds are large, and the distance between plants 3 ft.

There are vegetable sowings to be made outside, when we can find the time, getting in a large patch of broad beans, for later freezing, by the end of the month. Peas usually wait till early May. They seldom relish our cold, heavy soil before that.

Bamboos are on the move again. It is the phyllostachys that come through the winter looking smartest at a time when evergreens in general are notoriously tatty. But you can help your bamboos enormously by thinning out each colony at this season. Make yourself comfortable on a kneeling mat (if you're sensible and not one of the proud stooping-only idiots), and methodically cut out, as low as you can so as not to leave stumps that will get in your way on future occasions, all the old canes that have become weak and unlovely (some will actually be dead) with age. This will open out a clump so that you can see between its canes, which is a great improvement. It will be removing all the least sightly growth and it will be making room for new canes. As always, pruning, especially in spring, should go hand in hand with feeding. A compost mulch, for instance.

With some of the smaller bamboos like *Arundinaria viridistriata*, the best course is to cut all canes right down to the ground. Their young shoots are by far the freshest and brightest in colouring. Once they have started shooting, you can dig up pieces of bamboo clumps and pot them. It is safest to start them in a close frame or greenhouse. Spring is also the time for splitting, moving and re-establishing any ornamental grasses that need this treatment.

Shrubs to think about now are the winter-flowering mahonias. Nearly all of them are naturally leggy, and all need looking over with a view to shortening quite severely and into old bare wood any branches that have developed bare stems. Wherever you make your cut new shoots will arise, and you won't lose any blossom next winter, so timidity is out of place.

It is against this background of activity that I can now write about the garden's highlights in a more relaxed vein. However busy you are, you should always take some daytime minutes off for complete relaxation because that recharges your batteries for further action. Besides, you're not living if you never stop to look and listen.

I find the best time and place for this is after lunch, by the Horse Pond. The slope overlooking it faces north and isn't sunny enough before April, but from now till the end of September it is, and there's the shade of a red oak for when the sun becomes too hot. Often, when I take my coffee out, there's a heron fishing. I don't know whether it finds the goldfish easier to see, and therefore catch, than the mud-coloured kinds. The goldfish are particularly prominent in early spring and are at the surface on sunny days to bask, but they are extremely wary.

Not so the grass snakes, more sensibly called European water snakes, which is what they are. There are usually two of them – one takes scarcely any notice of me, the other is more inclined to slip away if I come close, so I usually don't. They bask on the stems of one of the ling plants that overhang the pond, and can be seen most days from now till early August.

There are frogs and toads about too (what a satisfying noise their croaking is), evidently enough of them for spawning before the snakes have made their breakfast off them. I once, by the margin of the Sunk Garden pool, came upon a snake in the act of attacking a toad. I interfered and released the toad, which was already wounded, and I don't know if it recovered. I decided after that never to interfere again. What business is it of mine to arbitrate? It's too easy to think you've done a good deed by interfering, when you've done nothing of the kind.

There is often a tree creeper to be seen among the birches, from my vantage point, and a moorhen or two on the pond. They are pretty unconcerned, but the water is still too short of cover to risk a first brood here. That will be on a more secluded pond nearby, close to the farm buildings. We shall get our young family later on.

Here dead gunnera leaves form the setting for snakeshead fritillaries
and many other spring bulbs, which can complete their cycle before the gunnera's
own foliage fully expands and darkens all beneath it.

Left: water saxifrage, *Darmera (Peltiphyllum) peltata,* competes happily with dogwood and willow (by the Horse Pond) if the latter are stooled every other year.

Right: A large and showy kingcup, *Caltha polypetela,* will grow in water as well as on the margin. It is one of the first flowers to liven up the Horse Pond.

The greatest excitement is when the first swallow or pair of swallows arrive. As often as not, I see them in our kitchen yard, by the open-sided shed that holds our fuel oil tanks, above which they nest (my mother called it the Black Hole of Calcutta). But if it's by the Horse Pond there'll be aerobatics, because the swallows cannot resist dipping into and skimming over the water from various angles. It is a great symbolic moment. Winter is really behind us at last. If one swallow doesn't make a summer, it certainly makes a spring.

The gunneras (*Gunnera manicata* and *G. tinctoria*) begin to unfold their leaves surprisingly early; I suppose they need time in which to deploy their great expanse of sail. If the first leaf in each crown is frosted, as it often is, no matter. Others unfold successively, like Banquo and all his descendants in Macbeth's disturbing apparition. But they are so slow about it that all sorts of small plants have time to complete their growth cycle within the territory of this monster, where all will later be in darkness *(p. 61)*. There are winter aconites, snowdrops, anemones, Lent lilies, fritillaries and, latest of all, self-sown spotted orchids in June, but still the gunneras are not in full fig.

The water saxifrage, *Darmera* (*Peltiphyllum*) *peltatum*, tries to behave like a mini-gunnera, flowering first above naked rhizomes, then sending up its own umbrella leaves. But the flowers are beautiful Easter bonnets of pink blossom supported by fleshy pink stems, which are covered in coarse bristles. The earliest kingcup, white version of *Caltha palustris*, was out last month. Now it is the turn of *C. polypetala*, whose first blooms are really large and splendid, single yellow affairs. This will grow under water and even needs reducing, from time to time.

Meanwhile, in wet places near the pond, the lady's smocks are in full bloom, and there'll be Orange Tip butterflies (which feed on them) on the wing before the end of the month. Brimstones will be putting in an appearance – they are great travellers – and the Holly Blue, pale and ethereal, but sometimes I don't see this until its second brood has hatched in August.

Other areas of meadow are rich in snakeshead fritillaries, *Fritillaria meleagris*, checkered purple or white or some intermediate shade. They love our heavy soil and keep increasing. Then there are proud spikes of early purples, *Orchis mascula*, above heavily spotted foliage. My mother and I originally introduced these from the woods, but they have taken over and now occur in many areas where we never thought to plant them. This is the kind of immoral outcome which conservationists cannot bear to contemplate (not in public, anyway).

The early purple orchid, *Orchis mascula,* was originally introduced by us from nearby woodland and now self-sows in every piece of meadow at Great Dixter.

I shall not omit to mention the dandelions, which need no introducing, but what a wonderfully rich shade of yellow they are. They quickly run to seed, but, before ripening, the goldfinches pull the seed out in tufts. You can always see where they've been. We have pink, pale blue and white Spanish bluebells in the grass – they all mix well – and patches both here and (less welcome but no less beautiful) in some of the borders of our native bluebells.

The biggest and largest established patch of the so-called summer snow-flake, *Leucojum aestivum*, grows at one end of the Upper Moat and is in full bloom by early April, pretty well finished and flattened by the end. It grows like a daffodil. This is the South European strain, which is the commonest in cultivation, but its white, green-tipped bells are much smaller and less telling than those of 'Gravetye Giant' which, I am informed, is none other than our native strain, sometimes called Loddon lily (the Loddon being a tributary of the Thames). It will put up with any amount of wet – drowning, even – and I have it pretty well swimming among our dogwoods by the Horse Pond. It looks good with their carmine stems, though some of these were stooled early in the month so as to encourage young growth, which has the strongest colour. 'Gravetye Giant' is later flowering than the usual type and runs on into May *(p. 74)*. It never flops.

The slopes are terraced in many parts of the garden, and the retaining walls are all colonized by aubrietas. Their soft mauves and purples are fresh and lively, and their untrimmed pendulous cushions have none of the self-conscious primness that one is aware of in gardens where they are properly looked after. Neither do we alternate purple aubrieta with mustard yellow alyssum – a smashing plant in itself but the contrast is a bit noisy. Make it just once and we'll get the message without needing to see it repeated over and over.

A gentle contrast to aubrieta is the pale yellow of primroses, and these will grow in dry walling very happily. Another successful contrast, which happened here by accident along our back drive, is aubrieta with the light green flower heads of *Euphorbia robbiae*. Normally you plant this spurge as ground cover in shade; it will even tolerate dry shade. But in this instance it has colonized by self-sowing in as dry and sunny a spot as could be found, and it has run through the wall cracks as though this was where it had always longed to be. Furthermore, its inflorescences at midsummer take on an attractive coppery hue, which never happens in shade.

On the south side of the house aubrietas can be seen in the same eyeful, so to speak, as a blush *Magnolia stellata* – daffodils in the background – and that looks good too. A number of magnolias are flowering now and *stellata* is the

Euphorbia robbiae has sown itself to join aubrieta on a sunny retaining wall.
Sun suits this spurge as well as shade, and turns its dying inflorescence to
warm coral shades in early summer.

earliest, usually showing before the end of March. Its flowers are vulnerable
to frost and wind like any other magnolia's, but they open over a period of
several weeks and so the shrub shows considerable resilience. I now have the
excellent *M. × loebneri* 'Leonard Messel', a hybrid between *M. stellata* and *M.
kobus*. It flowers in early youth, it grows strongly, and its colouring is a more
definite shade of pink than you usually find in *M. stellata*. One could scarcely
ask better.

Near to 'Leonard Messel' and given plenty of elbow room, because I
realized from seeing the parent plant that it would have wide elbows, I have

M. × veitchii 'Peter Veitch'. It flowers for ten or fourteen days in April, and you keep your fingers crossed for windless weather because it can be sadly battered and there's no redress. But such is the cussedness of human nature that we actually enjoy the unreliable plant in its occasional moment of glory more than all the steady rent-payers put together. We watch and we wait in hungry anticipation – magnolias give you plenty of scope for that because their flower buds can be seen and counted from way back in the previous autumn – but we should not curse our luck if things go awry. Nobody's interested in other people's bad luck (except as an excuse to recount their own); it's just a bore.

This magnolia has large goblets of a light but definite pink. There's usually some imperfection when you look closely at one. Either half close your eyes or stand back and take in the general display – against a blue sky, naturally. (I had a *Paulownia* once; an exciting tree relation of the foxglove with clusters of purplish funnels in April before the leaves expand. But I could never see them. They always seemed to be displayed against a slaty grey sky which didn't show them up as anything better. I was relieved when it died.)

At the bottom of our Long Border is a small group of *Magnolia denudata* (known as *M. conspicua* at the time the garden was made and they were planted). I have mentioned them in connection with the aucubas and hellebores that grow beneath them and I can add a number more to this tally of protégés: *Crocus tomasinianus*, *C. speciosus*, *Narcissus* 'February Gold', *Geranium endressii*, *Cyclamen hederifolium*, *Campanula poscharskyana*, *Vinca major* 'Alba', *V. difformis*, *Danaë racemosa*, and a stranded bearded iris from the early days when it grew around yuccas *(p. 11)*. Its colouring my mother described as French grey. It is now a useless, sentimental piece of lumber. The magnolia is pure white and lemon-scented. The best view of it for the few days that it is blooming is looking down from my bathroom window. Indeed, the reflected glare noticeably illuminates the bathroom.

Best of my magnolias is another old steady from the garden's earliest days: *M. soulangiana* 'Lennei'. It has large, deep purplish pink and incurved blooms, about the size and shape of a 150-watt electric light bulb. When you tap the fleshy petals they make a gentle, hollow sound. It has a sprawling habit, so it is just as well that it grows against a high terrace wall, but not entirely. One branch has spread outwards across a piece of paving that

Opposite: *Magnolia soulangiana* 'Lennei', beneath whose branches
Scilla bithynica was flowering a few weeks ago *(p. 52)* The magnolia's lax habit
is given partial support against the terrace wall.

doesn't have to be trodden, so I have left it. You can look down into its chalices for a change, like catching a recumbent giant in his sleep.

Next to this grows *Azara microphylla*. Its tiny yellow flowers are so inconspicuous that nobody notices them except by their extraordinarily far flung vanilla scent. Seldom is this traced to its origin.

The other scent that currently wafts half-way round the garden on the other side of the house is from the four osmanthus bushes in the Barn Garden. I mentioned them in my Introduction *(p. 12)*. I have never managed to take a satisfactory photograph of them yet and thus conclude that they are not photogenic shrubs, but they rather nicely highlight any earlier-flowering tulip that may be near them. I'm particularly fond of the long blooms of a Fosteriana hybrid, 'Orange Emperor'. Wind generally plays havoc with them within a few days. Enclosed gardens like this and the adjacent Wall Garden are deceptive. They look sheltered but in fact the walls cause vicious turbulence. You don't find this with hedges, which can absorb much of the wind that strikes them.

There's quite a lot going on in the Sunk Garden/Barn Garden enclosure. Blue periwinkles (*Vinca minor*) on the floor of the Sunk Garden and wads of white or yellow encrusted saxifrages on its retaining walls. I should add to and replace some of these but tell myself I haven't the time. Inserting new plants firmly into dry walling isn't easy. I tend to give rein to those that will seed themselves between the cracks, or else run about from an initial planting on the wall top (infested with ants, however), as will *Campanula portenschla-giana* and *Geranium dalmaticum*.

In the Barn Garden above I have the pink blossom of the suckering dwarf almond, *Prunus tenella*, and of its more richly coloured, larger-flowered clone, 'Firehill'. The latter should be the better, and I think, while still in bud, it does look more exciting, but the flowers themselves are coarsened and none too well shaped. In the aggregate I lean to the type plant but am pleased to have both.

Another bush prunus, the double white *P. glandulosa* 'Alba Plena', is wreathed with blossom now. The flowers readily brown from a fungus disease, but a timely watering with Benomyl checks this. Next to it the deep blue, fine-leaved rosemary, *Rosmarinus officinalis* 'Benenden Blue', which Cherry Ingram introduced from Corsica and which I was originally given as cuttings from Sissinghurst Castle by Vita Sackville-West. Once established, I

Opposite: Lichens, seen here on Lutyens's circular steps,
are particularly prominent in the spring and make oyster patterns.

The forget–me–not–like *Omphalodes cappadocica* is a perennial that will
put up with a lot of shade. Here it grows in front of *Spiraea japonica* 'Goldflame',
which has its brightest leaf colouring in the spring.

don't believe that this strain is any less hardy than ordinary rosemary. I positively like its sprawling habit because you can grow other things between its branches. I have, for instance, a deep pink clone of avens, *Geum rivale* (from Mrs Fish). It comes out now and so does *Salix hastata* 'Wehrhahnii', a male bush willow with cuddly pussies. Each of these is subtended by four furry bracts which stick out like ears. Across the path are two huge clumps of my favourite spurge, the herbaceous *Euphorbia palustris*. It epitomizes the freshness of spring, and if you catch the light right on a sunny evening, the flowers sparkle as though there was a tiny glass crystal in the centre of each.

In another damp and partly shaded border grows the double form of Canadian bloodroot, *Sanguinaria canadensis*, whose white flowers open like little waterlilies in the sun. They are only a few inches high and each is wrapped around its stem by a scalloped leaf, which expands later. Self-sown forget-me-nots nearby make a pretty contrast but I have to guard against them swamping their precious neighbours.

Spiraea japonica 'Goldflame' is a handsome newcomer on the gardening scene. Essentially this is a foliage shrub, the young leaves rich copper, gradually fading over the next two months to lime green. I think it looks well with the rich blue of *Omphalodes cappadocica* planted in front. Like a perennial forget-me-not but larger. You need a good strain of this plant, such as I was given by Cherry. It will flourish in amazingly deep shade, for example under a rhododendron or a camellia.

The Long Border has little flowering in it yet apart from tulips and grape hyacinths, so you can turn aside, at its top end, to look across the countryside, with a soft green haze from larch woods in the middle distance, to Tufton Place beyond. There, alas, the six-cowled oast house unit has been burnt down, but the house is handsome. This, across an unplanted piece of our orchard, is the one view that I allow from the garden, because it looks to the south and south-east, and no damaging winds come from that direction. Otherwise the best view we have is looking north from the top car park, across the rolling field, now full of sheep and lambs, called Great Park, to the thirty acres of Weights Wood, where green is rapidly coming into the hornbeams which comprise the main underwood in this district. There are birches, too, coming into young leaf at the same time as their catkins expand. There are no elms or beeches in the area, other than those planted in gardens or along roads. Our only beech stands behind the potting shed and was planted by my mother as a seedling. It is a great moment when its buds explode into their amazing pageant of new green, somewhere about the third week in April.

Spare a glance to your left as you approach Dixter at the turn of this month and next. You may see me grubbing cow parsley plants, which can be pulled intact when flowering, but longer on the scene is a *Rhododendron* × *loderi* 'King George', with loose trusses of pale pink in which each bloom is five inches across. Size here goes with an unbuttoned, carefree habit and a strong fruit scent. I also have a planting of the vivid magenta azalea, *R. obtusum* 'Amoenum', and I wish I had more still. It is incandescent beneath the trees.

There is a north-facing bank here – a legacy of the iron ore workings I mentioned *(p. 16)* – and it is covered with self-sown ferns which Albert Croft has always been careful to leave intact when cutting grass, brambles and other rubbish on the bank once a year. But in April there are more precocious ferns in the garden itself. Adiantums are always up before I expect them. There's a long-established colony of *Adiantum pedatum* 'Klondyke' in a border in the High Garden which has no protection from the sun (any protective shrub I plant behind it either dies or turns out to be wrong for that spot), and yet its transparently delicate young fronds come to little harm. The other hardy maidenhair is *A. venustum*, which makes a low sward. The oak fern has the same slowly colonizing habit. That is *Gymnocarpium dryopteris* – an excellent filler between a path and a hedge bottom, as you see it at Sissinghurst. Hartstongues and shield ferns will have had their old evergreen fronds cut away last month so as to make room, without damaging them, for the young croziers. In *Polystichum setiferum* 'Acutilobum', they unfurl with the vigour of a bunch of serpents rising from the ground. Another snaky-looking plant at this stage – a spotted snake – is the dragon arum, *Dracunculus vulgaris*, only in this case the young shoots resemble adders disappearing into the ground, only their tails remaining. These are located behind the blood-roots in the Barn Garden, and here also is a colony of woodruff, *Asperula odorata*. I think its heads of tiny cruciform flowers look whiter than white because of the very pale green of the leaves that surround them. Albinos often have pale leaves and it adds to their freshness.

There's another fern that will lead me into another subject, the creeping haresfoot, *Davallia mariesii*. Although it receives gingerly treatment by those (not many) who grow it, this is perfectly hardy and will thrive in sun or in shade. Nine inches high at most and with bipinnate fronds, it makes charming cover from spring to October, when it changes to pale rust before shedding.

I have it also in an earthenware trough-pot, and it stands outside our front porch all through its season. Here from now on I stand pots of various things that I have grown in the greenhouse or frames, to make a welcoming group when they are flowering. Daffodils and narcissi; *Fritillaria pallidiflora*, with

From spring to autumn, welcoming pots of flowers stand outside our front porch. *Iris bucharica* is on the right, and wallflowers self-sow in the fern border on the left.

pale green bells; *Anemone blanda*, especially the robust and showy 'White Splendour'; the florist's genista (*Cytisus fragrans* or whatever you like to call it); and the Juno iris, *Iris bucharica*, which has yellow and white flowers among glossy foliage. There are also, in April and early May, pots of *Gladiolus tristis*, which I'm crazy about, but most of these go into the house to scent the rooms at night with their lemony fragrance. The elegant little flower spikes are in shades of pale green.

Before I leave April, I must say a kind word on behalf of the mosses and lichens, which are at their liveliest now. The several kinds of lichens on the York stone paving have an appliquéd look, especially around the margins, where they are sporulating most freely *(p. 69)*.

The lawns are full of moss – I don't attempt to eliminate it and they are lovely and spongy to walk on, like a deep-piled carpet; the colour a bright yellow green. Mosses are also dominant beneath oaks on the poor sub-soil close to the entrance drive, where I have made homes for rhododendrons and a few azaleas. 'An appreciation of moss is a sign of maturity,' Archie Skinner once said as we were walking round Sheffield Park Gardens. True, there are some people who have to come round to them, but I cannot remember when they didn't give me pleasure.

May

---◆---

THE very word, short and direct, seems full of light and ready to become airborne. Man compares himself with the world around him, with the birds shouting their songs, the trees bursting into leaf; old or young, in imagination or in fact, he feels himself a part of this great creative impulse.

> Im wunderschönen Monat Mai, als alle Knospen sprangen,
> da ist in meinem Herzen die Liebe aufgegangen,

wrote Heine at the start of his *Dichterliebe*, unforgettably rendered for voice and piano by Schumann.

The poet's love affair, which started in May, ended in bitterness and recrimination when he was jilted. We're not told which month that happened, but it must have been November, for sure, when the leaves were falling. Those who sing the praises of May most highly are the same who revile autumn as depressing. But I think if you have a gut sympathy with the natural cycle of the year, the charms of autumn are as vital as the forward impulse of spring.

The whole countryside, manmade though it be, is so beautiful in May that there is scarcely need for a garden. Just walk about – or drive, if the air is horribly cold – and stare. I have no horse chestnut in my garden, but yours or the one standing by the village green will give me the thrill I wouldn't miss. What a wonderful confection, piled high on its vast dome and glittering against a storm cloud. There is no flowering tree to touch it. I mean the white chestnut, of course; the red entirely lacks its charisma.

Trees are to the fore this month. There being little space for them within our garden, it is the oaks on our north-east and south-west boundaries that I most admire, in their yellow-green freshness. They make a good backdrop. North-eastwards they line the approach to Dixter. South-westwards and providing essential shelter from the prevailing winds, they comprise a

Opposite: New foliage on the oaks. They are set well back from the Horse Pond, at whose margin these snowflakes, *Leucojum aestivum* 'Gravetye Giant', flourish in sopping wet ground among the dogwoods, *Cornus alba*.

narrow slip of woodland behind the Lower Moat, which is our second pond, totally different in mood from the Horse Pond.

These oaks are growing in the spoil from the moat when it was dug, and although that was more than 500 years ago, it is still only subsoil at best, parent clay at worst. The oaks manage well enough; so do primroses, but it is difficult to persuade shrubs to flourish beneath the trees. My father planted a row of hybrid rhododendrons here. They never grew particularly well, but two have survived in reasonable health. The brash pink 'Cynthia' is one. Flowering mid-month onwards, I sometimes find it useful, stripped of its leaves, in a flower arrangement for the Great Hall – perhaps with purple 'Souvenir de Louis Spaeth' lilac and the huge blood red oriental poppy, 'Goliath'.

The other rhododendron is more interesting. It flowers earlier, in April–May, and its slender leaves are far less clumsy than the generality of hardy hybrids. From seeing it and having it named for me in Sheffield Park Gardens (thirty-five miles west of here), I'm glad to know that this is *Rhododendron* × *baddaertianum*. Again nice to pick; a soft pale pink.

The Lower Moat is a dark, unreflecting piece of water entirely overhung by oak branches. In respect of water gardening, this is a poor arrangement with one outstanding exception. A *Gunnera manicata*, also planted around 1930, develops the most enormous leaves in half shade. It is the public's darling, and a track is quickly made in the lengthening grass around it by visitors being photographed underneath its umbrella.

Other waterside plants that will thrive in shade are osmunda ferns; our native flag, *Iris pseudacorus*; and the so-called skunk cabbage, *Lysichitum americanum*, with yellow arum spathes in spring. I have had great difficulty in establishing it anywhere.

The moat was entirely obscured by green duckweed in the early 30s, and my mother said that the only way to get rid of it would be with ducks. The idea appealed to me enormously. Without informing my father, who would not have given his sanction – a *fait accompli* was the only solution – we bought two hybrid ducks, Jemima and Vashti, and a hideous drake, Puddledrake, in the village. We had them and their offspring for several years, and they were followed by Aylesburys, and they by Khaki Campbells. The duckweed disappeared in quick time. After the war we gave up most of our livestock and I would not have them back. The flat feet of ducks around a pond are not helpful to precious plants. Meanwhile the duckweed remained in abeyance *until*, in 1985, more than fifty years after, it made a return and completely coated the moat again. I can't say it worries me any longer.

Gunnera manicata stretching itself.
The cone-like inflorescence is most prominent before the leaves have fully expanded.

The old wild pear, *Pyrus communis,* was here before the Lloyds.
Its scent carries far on the air. The dome shape is echoed by *Chusquea culeou,*
a Chilean bamboo which replaced a yew topiary specimen in the lawn.

But the workings of this aquatic are mysterious. We have it – two species of *Lemna* have been identified – in very small quantities around the margins of the Horse Pond, but it has never taken charge there.

It is by the Lower Moat that I often see the first spotted flycatcher of the year, using one of the overhanging oak branches as base for its fly-catching. I wish I could still hear the snap of its beak. Although there is a great deal of birdsong in and around the garden (far more than in the surrounding countryside), I do miss the chiff-chaffs, whitethroats and lesser whitethroats that used to be regulars, while willow warblers are only occasional. I think they may be returning. Cuckoos are about, but not invariably in or close to the garden as in former times.

Woodland gardens are at their climax in May, but Dixter is nowhere near it yet. However, there are two substantial dollops of blossom in the first half of the month. Bullfinches take no notice of 'Bramley's Seedling' apples, nor of certain pears. The Bramleys are big trees, planted in the early 1920s, and this apple is one of the prettiest and pinkest as it comes into flower. Although at the top of the garden and near our boundary, they show up well when you walk out of the front door and look half right.

Much closer – right in front of the house, indeed – is a wild pear of enormous size that predates the Lloyds at Dixter. It grows now through the centre of one of my father's yew hedges. He used to have it clipped every year so that it looked like a shaving brush at the end of each growing season. It never flowered. By 1947 my mother and I decided that it (and we) had had enough of this boring treatment and it has been allowed to grow freely ever since. Within two or three years of the start to its new life, our old faithful flowered, and it has flowered unfailingly ever since; a vast cumulus cloud of blossom wafting that delicious sickly pear scent far and wide. Its display, around 5–10 May, lasts for five days, which is as much as you can expect from most blossom.

Such another is the *Malus floribunda* planted by the oast house, where no one would see it except that it has now overtopped the Wall Garden wall so that its crown makes a lovely pink cap, sitting on the wall as seen from the porch when you look left. It is in the bud and early blossoming stage that this crab is beautiful. Once in full bloom, it bleaches and looks tired.

We have a clutch of 'John Downie' crabs (the best for jelly but even then not too exciting) in front of the house that change quickly from blush buds to a good solid white, and they are a picture, briefly. In the orchard behind the house I have planted quite a number of *Malus hupehensis* that I raised from seed, from which, thanks to apomicty (the capacity to set seed without fertilization), it comes true. Blush pink buds open to unexpectedly large white blossom. This species, one of the latest in flower, makes a lovely tree in time with good bark. I look forward to that.

On the other side of the front path from our old pear is a bay laurel, *Laurus nobilis*, of the same age. It is a bulky object, a male (our neighbours have females and we often find bird-sown seedlings in the garden), and it flowers abundantly now. Little yellow puffs which scent the air when the weather is kind.

It seems odd to write of roses almost in the same breath as spring blossom, but things happen quickly in May with every day bringing a new first. The single yellow *Rosa hugonis* types have let me down too often with the die-back disease that they are prone to and which soon kills them. No more 'Canary Bird' for me, but *R.* × *cantabrigiensis* is a good substitute with a healthy constitution. I have two plants on their own roots (they strike easily) and they are covered briefly with creamy yellow single roses, deliciously scented on the air. Their lacy foliage continues to look quietly pleasing all through the summer.

R. primula, with its remarkable incense smell, especially after rain, does keep dying back on me but recovers by suckering from its own root stock. I can occasionally divide it but have not succeeded with cuttings – a rare and somewhat mortifying case. It flowers, wanly, now.

Our native *R. pimpinellifolia* (*R. spinosissima*) is usually found in the wild within smell of the sea. As it grows in very poor soil it is only a foot or so tall and one wishes that it would stay compact in the garden. It tends, however, not only to straggle but to run incontinently. The best place for it is between the cracks of paving. Its cream flowers are followed by almost black hips. It has sported to many colours and to numerous doubles. I have a double pink, a double yellow and the double magenta 'William III'. This grows at the top of the Long Border and has *Viola cornuta* 'Alba' growing into and through it. I like that combination with the leaves of *Alchemilla mollis* in front and of *Hosta sieboldiana* 'Elegans' to one side. They knit together well.

The viola is a great favourite that I have often written about; another albino with dead white flowers and pale green foliage. Given moist soil, it flowers on and on. When not too tangled among other plants, you can cut it back mid-season, which will encourage a second flush in late summer as fresh and free as the first was in spring.

I wrote of the Burnet rose as being a good paving crack plant where its wandering habit can be contained and its stature kept to the minimum. There are other crack plants in season now. I am never quite sure that *Sisyrinchium*

Viola cornuta 'Alba' flowers early and late and will thread its way
through any nearby low-growing shrub. The lady's mantle, *Alchemilla mollis,*
self-sows with embarrassing freedom, so I cut it to the ground in early August
and it soon refurnishes with young foliage.

angustifolium, the blue-eyed grass (yellow-eyed and not a grass) is worth it,
but there it is and unlikely to go away. A clumpy plant, it covers itself at 8
inches with small, iridaceous flowers that only open at lunchtime and on fine
days. If they were intense blue they would be thrilling, but the colour is
lustreless and the display soon over as they run to seed. There is a moment of
tepid pleasure when you sub-exclaim 'There they are in bloom', but the next,
they're not.

Cymbalaria muralis, the ivy-leaved toadflax, is a trailing perennial with
small mauve toadflax flowers. It grows in walls and paving and there is an
albino form which is pretty, too, and helps keep the atmosphere in my
greenhouse humid in summer, where it grows all over the benches. These
two have a continuous flowering season from spring to late autumn. So has
the little Mexican daisy, *Erigeron mucronatus*. We cut the old growth back in
early spring to neaten it up and away it goes, white daisies changing to pink as
they age. It is in every wall, step riser and paving crack untreated with
weedkiller. A charmer until late in the year when it becomes untidy again.

Another erigeron, *E. glaucus*, sometimes seeds into dry wall cracks and nowhere looks better. You never see this on sale yet it abounds in seaside gardens – loose curtains of mauve daisies with a large green eye.

Spring bedding is at its best in May, and I vary it from year to year, repeating myself only at long intervals if at all. This, it seems to me, is one of the major interests, not to say excitements, in bedding out: that you can continually experiment and with a rapid turnover of material. Tulips, wallflowers, stocks, pansies and columbines all come into it. I have used geums, *Omphalodes cappadocica*, *Viola cornuta*, doronicums. I really forget all the things I *have* tried. Tulips among sweet williams or lupins give a spread of interest.

When I grow wallflowers, which is not every year, it is always in single colour strains, but I sometimes interplant one colour with another or else plant separate colours in large adjacent blocks. I always grow my own plants, to get nice large ones. The seed is sown in the brassica seed bed early in May.

My chief bedding-out area is in front of the house. There's another couple of narrow, north-west-facing beds against a cow house in the Topiary Garden, but also many other odd pieces of border where the bedded-out

Left: When I grow wallflowers I like them in blocks of one colour, and tulips – here the late-flowering 'Mrs John Scheepers' – in similarly bold adjacent groups.

Right: The lily-flowered tulip 'Dyanito' has persisted for more than twenty years in an undisturbed area of the Long Border.

The parrot tulip 'Orange Favourite' is certainly *my* favourite.
It too has lasted for many years in the Long Border.

plants can blend with permanent plantings. I hate beds that are cut out of lawns. If you want a formal area with bedding, do it properly with paving between the beds. Grass never looks right. It is insufficiently formal and its bright green is a too active colour.

As to *Myosotis*, the forget-me-not, I am quite happy with the plants that sow themselves from year to year in the borders. In the Long Border they give colour – for instance among herbaceous phloxes – long before its main season has started.

But the Long Border is by no means dull in May. Besides the touches of colour coming in from giant chives, tulips, the little five-spot, *Nemophila maculata*, *Gladiolus byzantinus* and such-like, there are riches in its foliage. Dickson's golden elm has leaves that grow in two ranks and overlap. They retain a brilliant freshness for many weeks. The cut-leaved golden elder, *Sambucus racemosa* 'Plumosa Aurea', starts coppery, then slowly lightens. *Euonymus fortunei* 'Silver Queen' is a green and white evergreen when it settles down, but in May the new superimposed foliage is lemon and green. This low, spreading shrub looks good in front of the rich purple shoots of *Clematis recta* 'Purpurea'.

The deep green pinnatifid leaves of *Papaver bracteata* 'Goliath' are seen in front of the cardoon, *Cynara cardunculus*, which is similarly shaped but glaucous and vastly larger. Great green glabrous moon leaves clothe *Crambe cordifolia*, which is throwing up its branched inflorescence at the rate of knots. The spikes of the foxtail lily *Eremurus robustus* grow several inches a day till they reach 8 ft and explode into a galaxy of blush white stars. But its lush green foliage at ground level has been a harbinger of excitements to come for weeks past.

Many hostas are pristine, as yet relatively unharmed by slugs and snails. I like them with ferns; for instance *Hosta undulata*, elegantly white-variegated, in front of the plumy *Polystichum setiferum* 'Bevis'. Rounded leaves in front of rounded leaves also look well where *H. ventricosa* 'Aureomarginata' grows in front of the expanding bouquets of *Veratrum album*. Then, a successful idea lifted from Graham Thomas, I have the almost disconcertingly glaucous *Hosta* 'Buckshaw Blue' in front of the still crinkled, purplish finger leaves of *Rodgersia pinnata* 'Superba', a plant which remains in beauty till late autumn. Behind them, *Euphorbia palustris* is still in flower, with a tendency to sprawl after rain.

Variegations are not always at their best in youth: *Elaeagnus pungens* 'Maculata' is dowdy on its young shoots, but youth generally suits the perennials. *Astrantia* 'Sunningdale Variegated' with *Lamium maculatum* 'White Nancy', for instance. The astrantia has a green and white palmate leaf. The dead-nettle is green and white too, the best of its kind so far, knocking 'Beacon Silver' and 'Chequers' each into its own cocked hat. The flowers of 'White Nancy' are white, too, which is helpful and lights up the kind of shady spot these plants enjoy.

The comfrey with big green-and-white leaves, *Symphitum* × *uplandicum* 'Variegatum', has a double season. Now is its first. It quickly runs up to mauve-blue flowers and still remains pretty but then has to be cut to the ground, whereupon its second foliage season – a far longer one – gets going in late summer and autumn as though it had come round to spring again. I must make a really bold planting of this excellent perennial.

Do you slightly despise Welsh poppies for being too common and free with their seedlings (which they certainly are)? But in the right place . . . Both the orange and yellow kinds are lovely fillers beneath and among hydrangeas in young leaf and even better among pinnate-leaved ferns.

Opposite: *Eremurus robustus,* one of the foxtail lilies, looks well in an architectural topiary setting. After flowering its site is taken over by nasturtiums.

Another excellent flower – monocarpic, this one – in shade is *Smyrnium perfoliatum*, often mistaken by flower arrangers for a spurge, but actually of the cow parsley family, *Umbelliferae*. It has the lime green colouring of a spurge, especially in its much enlarged bracts. Let it once seed and it will always be with you, just like the white-flowered honesty, *Lunaria annua*, which goes so well with it. Again, for the most luminous effect, grow it in the shade of trees or shrubs. If you keep this honesty separate from the other colours (and I like them and the variegated-leaved kinds too) it will come true from seed.

I am always trying to make plants look well together in their context, and sometimes things go right and perhaps I'll photograph them, but then there's a setback or a change for some reason and by the time I look at my photograph again it seems like ancient history – nostalgic history in some cases, progress in others. Nothing stays the same for long in a garden, until it becomes a fossil (or a National Trust property in some cases where they're determined to hark back to what they consider an important moment in its past).

I thought that *Euphorbia griffithii* 'Fireglow' should look pretty good with the rich lavender blossom of *Abutilon* × *suntense* behind and above it, but the wretched abutilon refused to survive in the required spot. Now I have the pale yellow broom, *Cytisus praecox*, instead, which isn't bad but the broom is none too happy. It's awfully heavy soil.

I have an early-flowering, low and clumpy Jacob's ladder, *Polemonium* 'Lambrook Mauve', and have given that for partner a pale yellow legume, *Thermopsis villosa* (which I have also bought as *T. caroliniana*). If and when the thermopsis takes to looking really pleased instead of faintly surprised, that should be a nice link-up. There are all too few *pale* yellow perennials.

Then I have, from Beth Chatto, a pink cow parsley, or that's what it looks like on a slightly more restrained scale. It is *Chaerophyllum hirsutum* 'Roseum', really a rosy mauve, which is almost the colour of *Geranium maculatum* (another Chatto gift), which I'm growing just in front, the border being shady. Further along I have the early globe flower, *Trollius* 'Canary Bird' (*pale* yellow again) with the tight white buttons of *Ranunculus aconitifolius* 'Flore Pleno'. However, the trollius flowers for such a short period that I'm trying to establish it in my semi-wild rhododendron area, where length of flowering matters less. Perhaps I shall one day have enough of it to do the same with *Arum creticum*, which I have in its yellow form. It flowers for about five days early in the month but is such an excitement that this short sell is readily forgiven.

Left: The globe flower, *Trollius* 'Canary Bird', with the nearly related *Ranunculus aconitifolius* 'Flore Pleno' in a shady border.

Right: Although it flowers for only a few days, the excitement of *Arum creticum* earns it willingly given space.

About ten days is as much as *Veronica gentianoides* gives you before its spikes become unbalanced. But the freshness of its pale blue colouring is exquisite, and I have as a carpet around it the lime-green-leaved form of creeping jenny, *Lysimachia nummularia* 'Aurea'. To end this saga: close to my kitchen and on the corner of a retaining wall there is a plant of the mauve, speckle-centred (like a cotton print) *Phlox douglasii*, and just behind it (pure accident, this) bushes of cooking thyme, *Thymus vulgaris*, whose flowering is simultaneous and whose flowers are exactly the phlox's colour.

One becomes very much aware of scents in the warmer weather that we hope for in May. It isn't yet warm enough to sit out in the evenings (I deliberately avoid the early weeks in Glyndebourne's picnic festival), so a night-scented shrub like *Daphne tangutica* or, with a spicier, sharper sweetness, *D. pontica*, should be planted close to where you have to walk between garage and house. It'll take your mind off your problems. *D.* × *burkwoodii* smells – of pinks – at any time of day. There are many kinds of lilac with a pleasant scent. I have *Syringa* 'Palibin' (latest name for you can guess what), which is a stiffly compact bush with lilac-coloured flowers; *S. persica* 'Alba', with gracefully arching habit to 5 or 6 ft, and I used to have *S. microphylla* 'Superba', with rich pink flowers and a double season, but that kept dying on me and I couldn't abide the insult.

In any case none of these smell as satisfying as the common old lilac, *S. vulgaris*. This also has the most numerous cultivars to choose from, and they all have the same scent. My biggest specimens in this group are double white 'Mme Lemoine' (unco stiff in the joints but I don't feel like turning the old girl out) and 'Souvenir de Louis Spaeth', which must be the most popular purple, single-flowered and not too heavy in the head.

Azara serrata is hardy enough to be grown as a wall shrub in most districts, but needs plenty of space. Its yellow blossom is quite showy, late in May, and smells deliciously of fresh fruit. That is near my kitchen door and has to compete on uneven terms with the odour of roast pork, from time to time. The Mexican orange, *Choisya ternata*, carries on the air, and I have even mistaken its scent for tobacco smoke, which can be worrying in a non-smoking household.

The first of the scented, climbing honeysuckles comes out late in the month: *Lonicera caprifolium*. It is charming with its disc-like perfoliate bracts supporting pale blossom, but is a once-flowerer and if, as in some years, the bullfinches have taken a fancy to its buds, there is nothing on offer. I have lost my largest and most ancient specimens of *Clematis montana*, first to the 1976 drought, then to the cold winter of 1985. Those that are left are strongly vanilla-scented on the air, especially as the flowers are going over.

Another climber that performs now is *Schizandra rubriflora*, which is hardy, quite rampant and seems to require no sun. It grows up the north-east-facing wall of the oast house. The buds hang like cherry stones on their stalks and open into waxy red flowers. The foliage is a bit overwhelming at this stage and the plant is more effective when fruiting in autumn. It is for its fruit that it has won an Award of Merit, but you need a male plant with your female. I have them intertwined, which is just as well as we do not appear to breed any enthusiastically pollinating insects. Perhaps Roy Lancaster, Tony Schilling or another of my more intrepid plant-hunting friends will hop along to Szechwan in the right season, some day, and see what's doing the pollinating job there. They could bring it back in a matchbox and release it at Dixter. It is noticeable that my lady is not nearly so fruitful where she is not entangled in her lover's embraces.

Wisterias get going in May, though I always think the warm quality of my favourite *Wisteria sinensis* scent belongs rather to summer than to spring.

The front of Great Dixter from the Barn Garden, showing the wisteria.

Our meadow areas are filling up with native flowers, now, as the grasses rapidly lengthen (and what a bind the lawn mowing is, but you can't stop grass from growing in England in May). Earliest of the grasses themselves to bloom are sweet vernal and meadow foxtail – this is one of the sweetest to pull and chew, like the best TV yokels.

All three of the principal meadow buttercups are into flower, first *Ranunculus bulbosus*, easily recognized without examining its bulbous root, by the way its green sepals bend back on to the flower stalk. Then the tall, widely branching *R. acris*, which is my favourite and I have the double form of it, which is very neat; and the giant semi-double 'Stevenii', reaching 4 ft in a border in the High Garden. The third is *R. repens*, which prefers the wettest places. It has chains of babies along runners like a strawberry's, and is a terrible pest when it mixes in with other plants in a border, as it readily does in a cottage-garden free-for-all. Not so bad as that at Dixter.

These yellows, always diluted, of course, with masses of green, are in startling contrast to red clover, now starting its season, as also are the yellow-centred, white moon daisies. You should always view them with your back to the sun, as they follow it.

Blue contrasts especially well with yellow and we have super colonies, inside the front gate, of *Camassia esculenta*, which would be like a bluebell except that its spikes are composed of stars. Not only does this clump up densely but it also self-sows. If the previous summer was hot, it flowers prodigiously; if not, there is quite a bit of blindness.

A lovely lot of green-winged orchis, *Orchis morio*, flowers this month. Its colouring is a cooler shade of purple than *O. mascula* and the spikes are smaller, but some of the colonies are dense. The most prolific has sited itself in the shallow turf that covers our reservoir, at the top of the garden, but that is somewhere you would have to seek out. There's plenty of it in the meadow area alongside our front path (but please don't tread down the grass) and more in the orchard.

Here, a large patch of the poet's narcissus or pheasant's eye, *Narcissus poeticus* 'Recurvus', will be flowering (though it has its off years), and if you search around its margin you will find the delightful little adder's tongue fern, *Ophioglossum vulgatum*, which used to be common in permanent pastures, but they no longer exist in my part of the country. The best locations for adder's tongues that I know of nowadays are in the machair of the Outer Hebrides.

May is our busiest month for customers visiting the nursery, though mail orders fall to a trickle and enter their close season, much to our relief, until the autumn. Potting off rooted cuttings continues, and there are cuttings to be taken, in particular of herbaceous plants like *Salvia nemorosa*, *Achillea taygetea* and monardas.

The seeds that were sown last month need pricking out and there are more seeds to sow; things like busy lizzies, zinnias, the related tithonias, dahlias for late bedding, cosmos and tagetes – both quick developers – cleome the spider flower, mallows to follow the lupins (especially *Malope grandiflora*), ornamental gourds (especially the turbans) and cucumbers to grow on last year's compost heap.

At last we get around to sowing a brassica seed bed in the open, and rows of peas; dwarf and runner beans, parsnips, turnips, beetroot, spinach – all the vegetables that you probably dealt with a month or six weeks earlier.

Our rhubarb bed, in which there are an early and a less early variety, is in full production, and I look for recipes that will make a change from the usual ways of serving it. (Unfortunately this is a 'fruit' that Jane Grigson cannot abide and she can hardly bring herself to write on it.) But the rhubarb also runs up to flower now and I insist on its being allowed to do so; it looks so handsome. My gardener's instinct is to cut them out, to save the plants (which don't need saving). I was furious one year when there was no blossom, but my one-man investigation revealed that in this particular season the rhubarb had entirely failed to flower.

Grigson is luckily at her best on gooseberries, and I hope to enjoy my first picking by 26 May. Earlier than this, the gooseberry sawfly, which also goes for my redcurrants, has hatched and laid its eggs, and its revolting larvae have started on my bushes. They are given a dose of lethal spray (no messing about with harmless remedies that don't work), and so the crop that follows needs thoroughly washing. There'll certainly be other hatchings of sawfly to deal with presently. If not, the bushes are entirely stripped of foliage.

A number of plants in the borders will need supporting. We are luckily placed in having woods around us that we coppice for firewood, and peasticks are the spin-off from that winter operation. It is the tops of the hornbeams that we save. I don't enjoy seeing a forest of sticks in position before they are needed, and so we tend to supply them as the necessity is becoming urgent – alstroemerias, *Clematis recta* (never was a plant less naturally erect), *Salvia* 'Superba', *Aster sedifolius* (*A. acris*) are examples. Others, with thicker stems and fewer of them, are more effectively treated with canes and fillis (soft string of a natural hemp colour). *Lychnis chalcedonica*, *Aconitum* 'Sparks's Variety', *Phlox paniculata* (the tall wild form) and *Asphodeline liburnica*, for instance. Oh, and delphiniums.

The last of the tender plants are turned out of the cellar, in particular cannas, hedychiums in pots and tubers of *Salvia patens*, though I also sow seed of this.

I often go away in early June, but before that I make a point of planting up the big ornamental pots that will later stand on the terrace where we sit out; also in and around the Sunk Garden. For the time being, and until the plants have knit together so as to be worth looking at, they stand in the frameyard where they are easily watered at the same time as everything else. Later on I have to rush around with watering cans (a job allocated to the garden boy in earlier days, when children left school at fourteen and weren't paid much).

By the end of May, the lupins are in bloom. The sight and scent of them persuade me that summer has arrived.

June

'WHAT is one to say about June,' wrote Gertrude Jekyll in the 1890s, 'the time of perfect young summer, the fulfilment of the promise of the earlier months, and with as yet no sign to remind one that its fresh young beauty will ever fade? For my own part I wander up into the wood and say, "June is here – June is here; thank God for lovely June!"'

A wood needs to have clearings where foxglove, campion and honeysuckle can flower if it is to be really enjoyable in June, for by now it is twilight beneath the trees and dangling tortrix caterpillars that have been making lacework of the oaks continually catch you on face and clothes. Miss Jekyll's wood was special; most woodland gardens will be on the brink of decay by now, unless they specialize in meconopses, primulas, astilbes and lilies. There's no wood here that I shall want to visit.

Dixter is a series of open enclosures. Here we have a build-up right the way through the month which will not reach its climax until July. That in particular applies to the Long Border; also to the Wall Garden; to a lesser extent elsewhere. I tend to concentrate many of my earlier May/June-flowering perennials and some shrubs in the High Garden.

This quite large area, entirely enclosed by yew hedges, yet stands for the most part open, especially to the south. It was laid out on the typical Edwardian principle for a food-supplying area of straight paths flanked by fairly narrow flower borders, these being backed by fruit espaliers ('Comice' pears, in our case), cordons or bushes, while the main areas behind these were devoted to vegetables. Nowadays, half the vegetables have been replaced by rows of flowers for cutting, of biennials being raised to bed out in the autumn and of plants for sale in the nursery. The two paths are at right angles and there is a central crossing with a paved area. On its corners there used to be bushes of washy pink hortensias – 'Mme Riverain', or something like.

No hydrangeas here now, but important features are called for, and these are mainly conifers and other evergreens like the comfortable *Hebe*

Opposite: Lupins grown from seed sown the previous year. They are discarded after flowering and replaced with annuals for a late summer and autumn display.

Tree lupins self-sow on this well-drained wall top,
last up to three years and then disintegrate. Their scent is delicious.

cupressoides 'Boughton Dome' (likened by one of my staff to a fat old lady sitting on a bus), shrubby euphorbias and a favourite grey, *Helichrysum splendidum*, which is remarkably hardy and which I keep young by cutting it hard back each spring.

The pear espaliers receive no attention other than having their young shoots spurred back each winter. They are covered in lichens; in places with clematis. Fruiting is spasmodic. I get some now and again but consider it as a bonus rather than a right.

Flowers show up well, and particularly eye-catching in early June as you walk up the steps from the Orchard Garden and through a gap in the yew hedges is the coming into view of a large mixed planting of Russell lupins *(p. 92)*. Lupins quickly become unsightly passengers if included in mixed borders having a later climax, but I love them too much to exclude them altogether. A garden the size of ours should have room for lupins. So I concentrate them here, but throw them out the moment their season is past. Meanwhile seedlings are being grown on for next year's display. If I want a change, I can bed out, in autumn, with something else.

There is a large and prolific aphid of lupins, both herbaceous and shrubby, that has reached us from America and become a pest in some years. It is protected by a thick wax coating and we have had to spray two or three times to clear it. That is a bore, but it does not happen all the time or on all the lupins.

Looking over the top of these you see a bush of the semi-single Kordes shrub rose, 'Fruehlingsgold'. A friend who had grafted it himself (he must have made a good job of it as I've never been bothered by suckers) gave it to me in the early 1950s and it always seems ready, if I regularly prune away the old, to produce plenty of strong young shoots.

Much more recent but extremely vigorous, and growing quite close to the lupins, I have the Holy Rose, which I like to call *Rosa sancta*. I had it from John Treasure's garden in Shropshire. I'm always sorry if I forget where a plant came to me from. Links with one's friends or the memory of them are

The unimproved oriental poppy, *Papaver orientale*. What better can you ask?

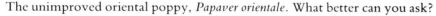

retained in this way. This is an early damask rose, a form therefore of *R. ×
damascena*, which seems to have originated in Syria and Asia Minor in the
fourth century A.D., was taken to Christian Abyssinia, where it was grown
in religious sanctuaries, and reached the west from there. Its pale pink single
blooms are set off by the purplish stalks that support them. It does not grow
taller than 4 ft, but is 9 ft across and would be more if I allowed it to self-layer,
which it readily does. But I sort it over each winter by removing all the
flowered branches, which are the ones that sink closest to the ground.

There are abundant oriental poppies in the High Garden, some red, some
white, but mostly the old-fashioned scarlet kind *(p. 95)*, and they look good
near the straightforward purple *Iris sibirica*, with the white star spikes of
Anthericum liliago in front. A cottage garden assortment. The iris would be a
nuisance in any quantity because, soon after flowering, its leaves become
overspreading in an outwards direction and behave execrably to lower
neighbours. This does not affect the poppies, which can themselves be cut to
the ground after flowering. You can then plant right up to and even between
their crowns with annuals.

Another good poppy that I have in the High Garden is *Papaver heldreichii*
(*P. spicatum*), a perennial that can be raised from seed to flower in two years. It
has softly felted grey-green foliage that holds dew and water drops and is
beautiful long before any flowers appear. Its carriage is stiff and upright to
$3\frac{1}{2}$ ft, and each stout stem is plastered with flower buds, either singly or in
threes. The first to open is at the top, working downwards from there. Where
there are triplets, the centre one opens first, the other two quite some time
later, so the season is spread out. The colouring of its crimped petals is soft
apricot. They all fall at midday, so I have to make sure I don't miss them.
Pretty to see *Thalictrum aquilegifolium* near this. I don't know the name of my
clone, which was a gift from a neighbour some thirty-five years ago, but it is
the most satisfactory I have seen, being only 2 ft high and having rich mauve
flowers, not washy, as they can be. Petals and sepals are vestigial or absent; it
is the powderpuff of stamens that makes the display.

Behind these two grows *Selinum carvifolium*, from Fish seed. It has the
laciest leaves of any umbellifer (parsley tribe) I know, and its white flowers
are entirely suitable though not always freely borne.

London Pride, *Saxifraga × umbrosa*, is an excellent carpeter around and
between other things and where you haven't yet thought of something you'd
prefer. It looks good in front of double crimson *Paeonia officinalis* peonies.
One of my London Pride colonies has been invaded by lilies-of-the-valley,
which turn out to be the more aggressive partner.

A dramatic flower arrangement can be made using *Papaver bracteata* 'Goliath'.
Newly opened blooms are picked in the morning, their stems boiled for twenty
seconds, and then they are given a couple of hours' drink in a deep florist's bucket
before I arrange them. They last five or six days in water.

Another carpeting infiller, in this case beneath bushes of the pink hybrid
musk rose 'Felicia', is the old-fashioned cranesbill that we used to know as
Geranium grandiflorum, now G. *himalayense*. It is deep blue and lovely for ten
days. After that you must be content with its foliage, which is good but not
so exciting that this deserves to be a front row plant.

I also have G. *endressii* 'A.T. Johnson' in the High Garden. Its pale pink
flowers are borne interminably and I wish I felt more grateful. They are at
their best early in the season before the plant sprawls unduly. It is a horrible
neighbour and I have reduced mine by three quarters. Even then it is wise to

cut it all back half-way through the season and make it start again. In front of this is a South African daisy, *Osteospermum jucundum*, a remarkably hardy, mat-forming perennial. Its rays are rosy mauve, the disc bluish. It has a tremendous floral outburst now but does not offer much later. If you cut it to the ground in spring you merely postpone the outburst to July.

My best colony of *Baptisia australis* is in the High Garden. With an obvious affinity to lupins, it has greater refinement. The flowers on its indigo blue spikes are quite widely spaced, not crowded, and its foliage remains fresh right through to autumn, not mildewing like lupins.

Another spiky flower in bloom this month is the slender *Eremurus bungei*, which is a rich yet soft yellow. I liked this with the comparatively short 'Blue Fountains' strain of delphinium, but they have not both done what they should in every year. Look out for them near Lutyens's charming (but now decrepit, so don't try to close it) little gate, leading out to the Horse Pond.

However, we must spend a little longer in the High Garden because there's a group I'm fond of, in rather more shade than most, close to the yew archway. This is dominated at the back by a particularly elegant (though not particularly hardy) bamboo, *Arundinaria falconeri*. So elegant that it is constantly attempting to weep over the path and, following rain, on to your clothes as you swish through it. This I counter (with only partial success) by cutting out, each spring, all its two-year-old canes, leaving only those that were made in the previous year. And I tie them loosely back to the espalier framework (taken over by *Rubus tricolor*) behind.

Underneath the bamboo are a fern of fresh yellow-green colouring that I brought back from Kashmir in 1971, *Polystichum fargesii*, some *Hosta sieboldiana* 'Elegans', with huge grey rippled leaves, and a patch of the double form of pink campion that grows wild in our woods, *Melandrium rubrum* 'Flore Pleno'. On the other side of the path the lyre plant, *Dicentra spectabilis*, and a monkshood, *Aconitum* 'Ivorine', which is quite short and, indeed, an ivory colour.

Now I must burst out of all enclosures, through the gateway that overlooks the Horse Pond, but also to a wide view of the Kentish landscape behind and even to the North Downs.

Immediately in front of me is a young red oak, *Quercus rubra*, which I was allowed to dig up as a seedling from underneath its magnificent parent in our

Opposite: *Geranium* 'Russell Prichard' flowers from May to November.
Like many other cranesbills it unifies a border's contents by infiltration,
as here, through giant chives.

neighbour's garden at Domons. That was around 1955. The parental tree broke up in a gale some years later, for this is a fast-growing North American species and not of the soundest. Its offspring, in poor soil, has grown fairly slowly but healthily. The bank beneath it is in shade, and ideal for reclining upon in the hottest weather. *Q. rubra* (syn. *Q. borealis*) has a handsome jagged cut to its leaves, which are tenderest lime green in spring; not specially exciting in autumn, but I'm not on the lookout for conflagrations. A steady glow is enough for me.

On the same bank as this tree are three deciduous species of *Elaeagnus*: *E. angustifolia*, *E. angustifolia caspica*, *E. umbellata*. The last of these is almost but not quite evergreen, and is all the better for losing its rather dull green leaves, but it is the first in flower. Next is *E. angustifolia caspica* and this is the handsomest bush with intensely silver foliage. Last to flower is *E. angustifolia*, which should, when happy, make a beautiful tree, easily compared with *Pyrus salicifolia*, to the latter's disadvantage. There's something wrong in this case, either with the strain I've planted or with the soil, which is horrible but the others don't seem to mind. So I have planted another youngster, ex Hungary where it is extensively planted and naturalized, in the orchard near the Long Border, and this seems to be getting away well.

The flowers in all cases are clusters of tiny four-lobed, buff-yellow bells with a most delicious spicy scent, opening in May–June. When I come out after lunch to drink coffee and stretch myself on the ground, I move my position from the neighbourhood of one bush to the next as their flowers open.

The Horse Pond has been transformed since I wrote of it in April. Masses of lush vegetation has grown up and the moorhens are rearing their second brood. The waterlily pads are constantly visited by pied wagtails, in search of insects among them, and by goldfinches and linnets, which come to drink. The banks of the pond are vivid with wild broom, which seeds itself. Each plant lives three years only, on average, but there are always more coming along. The weight of their blossom bends them to the water's surface and even under, which leads to stunning reflections. I also have *Genista tenera* (better known as *G. virgata*), the Madeira broom, here. This has a stiffer habit, a somewhat longer life and a silvery underside to its leaves. June is its season, and the flowers are much smaller than our own broom's but make up for that in quantity.

There is a great deal more of equally brilliant yellow from the flag irises, *Iris pseudacorus*, which grow abundantly in the shallow marginal water and also slightly above. It is a splendid plant that would be more ardently prized

The Horse Pond luxuriating in summer.

by gardeners were it not a native and almost too easily grown. But we are snobs. I have other irises emerging from the water, but lost the *laevigata* ones when we were treating the elodea with Diquat *(p. 40)*. Irises are particularly sensitive. However, I have 'Gerald Darby' here and also in the Sunk Garden. It is an extremely vigorous plant with fairly small, bluish flowers and purple stalks. Prolific, and nice the way its flowering stems are held at all angles from vertical to horizontal but the flower always faces upwards. I have also recently established the purple and white *I. versicolor* as an emergent aquatic, having moved it in from an ordinary border site. The idea came when I saw it growing, as though wild although it must somehow have been introduced, in a swamp in South Harris, where it was competing on equal terms with yellow flags. A little experimenting would, I am sure, reveal that many plants which we think of as wholly terrestrial are equally happy with their crowns under water, and this is such a pretty setting in which to see them. Other candidates would include *Lysimachia punctata*, *Schizostylis coccinea*, *Crinum* × *powellii*, *Monarda*, *Phalaris arundinacea* 'Picta' (ribbon grass) and *Lobelia cardinalis*.

Also *Senecio smithii*, which in the south of England is easiest to keep happy just under water, although in Orkney, where it is naturalized, it flourishes in the kind of places where you might expect to find a bed of stinging nettles – near a farm midden, for instance. Its domes of white daisies above glossy, hastate leaves open in June, here; a month later in the north.

I have an underwater island of white arum lilies, *Zantedeschia aethiopica*, which should be at their best this month and next but which have been through hard times with the weedkiller, so it'll be a year or two before they are fully re-established. But you can imagine how splendid their white spathes, seventy or eighty at a time, look in a watery setting.

The waterlilies themselves go from strength to strength through this month and next. The hotter the weather, the better they bloom (whereas the arums tend to scorch on a very hot day). The American hybrid 'Rose Arey' is the first to make its mark and has a clear, bright pink star-shaped flower. 'Escarboucle', the well-known crimson, follows and has the longest season, right into October. Then, a recent addition, there is 'Rose Magnolia', which is charmingly shaped, and finally the bowl-shaped 'James Brydon' which is purplish pink, very prolific but having the shortest season.

A flash of yellow that lasts for several months in the water below the dogwoods comes from Bowles's golden sedge, *Carex stricta* 'Aurea'. The damp meadow above this is thick with the spikes of spotted orchids, in shades of mauve, but there are many colonies throughout our meadow areas now, and their seed is so light that it carries far and wide. Any open piece of border left undisturbed for a few years becomes the home of *Dactylorhiza fuchsii* (*Orchis maculata*), and it also grows between paving stones in the Sunk Garden. The seeds do not ripen until late August, so it is worth leaving a piece of meadow where they grow uncut until then.

Meadow cranesbills, *Geranium pratense*, are abundant in late June and July, this being another wild flower that my mother would raise from seed and then spread around, but now it seeds itself. There is no improving its shade of blue, but I like the albino too, and have established that.

The vivid magenta of *Gladiolus byzantinus* looks super in grass, but the clone in general cultivation is sterile, so there is no self-seeding. But I grow a paler pink June-flowering gladiolus, which might be *G. segetum*, and this is fertile, so I have hopes. It is in the curious little arena surrounded by ilex

Our meadows are full of moon daisies, *Chrysanthemum leucanthemum*, but their numbers fluctuate mysteriously over the years. Certainly they love moisture.

hedges (*Quercus ilex*), which was originally designated a small formal garden surrounded by low yew hedges. The soil is the worst we have, and my mother did well to give the yews to my eldest brother for his garden when he married in 1934. I had a *Pinus patula* in the centre of this area, but it died following the 1986 winter. I fell in love with this Mexican species with its gracefully drooping needles in the pinetum at Wakehurst Place, forty miles to the west of Dixter. I'm really of the opinion that a piece of sculpture is what's called for here, but what piece? Nothing figurative seems right today (it's all been done before and better) and anyway I can't afford what a good sculpture would be worth.

In the orchard the moon daisies reach their peak quite early in the month. By the end, my favourite flower is the common bent grass, *Agrostis tenuis*, which makes a haze of pink and is especially happy in the open, unplanted area that looks out on a more distant prospect.

The Bourbon rose, 'Mme Isaac Pereire', has the best of all scents.
Its growth lends itself to pegging so that it makes horizontal garlands of blossom.

The Rose Garden keeps on deploying its forces until a grand climax is reached in the last day or two of the month and the first few days of July. Earliest are the Bourbons and hybrid perpetuals. 'Mme Isaac Pereire' outnumbers all others. Here is a rose that commands you to approach your nose to its ample bosom, but then rewards you with an even fuller scent than you had thought possible, though expectation ran high. (Mind the earwigs when you sniff.) The colour is bright, with a strong dash of magenta, but by no means harsh or tiring (as in 'Ulrich Brunner', which I have discarded). The oldest plant in the two beds devoted to this type of rose might be 'Candeur Lyonnaise', Graham Thomas thought. It came with my parents from their first garden, so it is nearly as old as the century. It throws very straight, bright green, almost thornless canes and the loosely double flowers are ivory white.

I have 'Easlea's Golden Rambler' in the centre of this bed, where it briefly makes amends for being a thoroughly cantankerous customer for the rest of the year. But I do like the soft yellows that were found in roses before the *Rosa foetida* influence became all-pervasive. I have it again in the single hybrid tea rose 'Mrs Oakley Fisher', which is soft apricot offset by purple stems. Vita Sackville-West started me on this with cuttings from Sissinghurst.

Opposite: The Rose Garden reaches a grand climax in the last few days of June.

In the days of my parents, each rose bed was devoted to one or two varieties, and when they faltered or went out of fashion they were replaced in a clean sweep. The beds in those days were edged with 'Maggie Mott' violas. In two of the central beds the last switch, around 1930, resulted in 'La Tosca' and 'Prince de Bulgarie' being replaced by 'Mme Butterfly', then at the height of its popularity. Since then I've worked on a piecemeal basis and have never replaced a bush if it continued to remain healthy. I still have some of those 'Mme Butterfly'.

It is an uncoordinated collection and yet there is a moment when I think it really is rather pretty. But there are more unplugged gaps than there should be. I always replant with my own rooted cuttings so as not to be bothered by suckers from an understock. Often the replacements fade out almost immediately (I take no precautions against replant troubles), but at other times they establish well. So it is a collection of the kinds of roses I like, or have liked but haven't the heart to get rid of, even though I've gone through them.

The peak season is very short because the Rose Garden becomes stifling in hot weather and nothing distresses roses more than being beaten on by unrelenting sunshine. You have to expect a dose of that in late June and early July. Dull, dry weather would be much kinder, but it rarely occurs at this moment in the year.

Nobody would dispute that this is a good time, but to get the weather just as we'd like it is not so easy. Too hot, and we shall moan that the roses are going over almost before they've opened. Too wet or chilly, and we shall exclaim 'Where is our summer?'

Evaporation is so rapid that plants will quickly show signs of distress. I'm a great believer in irrigation and I don't mind what time of the day the water goes on. The obvious disadvantage of midday watering is that the moisture evaporates so quickly, whereas if applied in the evening the plants will have had the chance to make good use of it before the sun is on the march once more. But if there's a drought I'll water from 6.00 a.m. to bedtime, moving the sprinkler every two hours. I have a card with SPRINKLER written on it that I put out in the bathroom so that I don't go to bed leaving it on.

The limitation is availability of water. We pump our own from a deep bore hole, and my father laid an irrigation system throughout the garden from the outset, which was enlightened of him. But the pressure and flow are not ecstatic and much is required in the nursery. That takes priority, so I have to fit other parts of the garden in when I can. The vegetables need water too. We get through 5,000 gallons or so a day, when the demand is fierce.

If I can, I follow up a watering with a weeding, as the weeds pull sweetly when the ground is soft.

The most implacable and hair-raising weed to cope with now is the lesser willowherb, a perennial that seeds itself like mad and makes a 3-ft plant in a twinkling. It only becomes relatively easy to spot when carrying its tiny pinky-mauve flowers. Walks round the garden with friends are apt to turn into weeding sessions, as you (and they) constantly dart into the borders in order to grab at some freshly spotted culprits. To catch the plants before they have seeded is the great idea, and for several weeks all goes well and you feel you're on top of the problem. Then, suddenly, you find you're not! As you pull the weed, a feathery haze of seed takes wing and you know that every one of that horde will germinate almost the moment it has touched down.

At least willowherb pulls easily. Sow thistles are apt to break off and, hydra-like, develop several heads where there was originally the one.

Probably goose grass, or cleavers, *Galium aparine*, is the most insidious of all annual weeds, because so easily missed until it is too late. Its flowers are only one tenth the size of the willowherb's and the plant's colouring blends into its surroundings. Also it has such a thread-like stem at ground level that, despite its voluminous and choking tophamper, it is difficult to be sure you have extracted the whole thing. More borders have been destroyed by goose grass than by bindweed. Once you have it, the problem will remain for ever. But you have to keep on trying. Turning a blind eye gets you nowhere, when it's your own weeds that are in question. You have to turn nothing less than your back, which is perhaps why I often go away in June – and later regret it.

I cannot leave the month without a bow to the common elder, *Sambucus nigra*, and its many variants. In the wild, its tumbling cascades of creamy flat-topped corymbs transform the most rubbishy dumps into places of beauty. And there is room for at least one elder in every garden. My biggest is cut-leaved, and it makes a tall column of blossom, not too far from the kitchen. This is the season for elderflower cordial. There are variants on the recipe. I like it as an entirely still, soft drink, so I put five or six large flower heads into a pan with four lemons, cut and squeezed, a pound of sugar and a gallon of boiling water poured on. After steeping for three days, this is strained into bottles and is ready to drink, chilled. Most refreshing.

July

---◆---

HERE we are in the hottest month of the year, and we must hope there's plenty of heat for us and the plants to make use of. Certainly my garden is at its most colourful in July, and that is probably because I grow a lot of hardy perennials, which tend to reach a peak now.

Mind you, I wouldn't advise anyone to visit the garden during the height of a July day. The circumstances are entirely unflattering. With short shadows and a white light, everything looks flat, limp and drained of vitality. It's a shame that the public has to see it like this. Only after they have left do freshness and depth of colour gradually return, though it is better still in the morning, up till about 11.00, when flowers are still benefiting from the night's coolth and dew.

At some stage in the month we shall be plagued by what people like to call thunder flies, actually tiny black thrips. They swarm in the air, and although they do not bite, they irritate by walking about over your skin and getting into your hair and on to your scalp. A thunderstorm at this point will wash them into deep drifts (a place at the foot of shallow steps into the Rose Garden is where I particularly expect to find them), and you can then see that they have a dusky bluish colouring.

We are not inordinately bothered by biting insects in this part of the country, but horseflies (clegs) can be a trial, especially when I'm picking raspberries in the cage. Many's the time I've rushed up and down the rows trying to escape a persistent tormentor.

So I am less inclined than in spring and autumn to take my writing things out into the garden in order to compose an article *al fresco*. More often I sit on the sofa in the Yeoman's Hall (the sixteenth-century addition to the house, not used in winter at all) with the door wide open on to the garden.

Even this practice has to be exercised with restraint, however, because the swallows are now looking for lodgings in which to rear their second broods,

Opposite: Myself posing in the Long Border. Left to right: *Genista aetnensis*, the Mount Etna broom; the rose 'Florence May Morse'; *Monarda* 'Cambridge Scarlet'; white *Phlox* 'Mia Ruys'; *Geranium* 'Russell Prichard' spilling on to the path.

and there's nowhere they would better like to occupy than a ledge in the roof of the Yeoman's Hall. The bats are much less trouble because they just come and go about their business as they please and can be ignored. They're in and out of the house all the time, sweeping around the bigger rooms, zooming up and down the passages and staircases. House guests simply have to learn to put up with their companionship. As in the bat house at nearby Glyndebourne, they're part of the scenario.

The belt of ash trees on the west boundary of our garden is at its most beautiful. Not that any of these trees has individual grandeur, but their silhouettes look buoyant against the evening sky. It is a part of high summer at Dixter, and greatly satisfying.

I said nothing about the Long Border last month, so must make amends, as it has been gathering strength for many weeks.

It is a border which evolves with the years. To a large extent it is the plants which dictate what shall happen next. Whether they suddenly do a lot better than you expected or suddenly start to falter and fail, it is up to me to take the hint and to apply flexible plans which can be modified as often as I like. I wrote 'suddenly' because changes are relatively swift, and it is surprising when I look at photographs taken, say, five years back, to see how much has happened. No feature that you have grown used to can be taken for granted.

I have a huge, almost tree-like specimen of the white *Escallonia* × 'Iveyi', near the top of the border. It is at the back, because I knew it would grow big, but I had no idea when I planted it just how big. It developed a tree form as I pruned the lower branches away so as to be able to go on growing other plants fairly close to its trunk. The escallonia is a wonderful white cloud of bee-besieged blossom for ten days in late July. Then it's over and becomes increasingly moth-eaten in appearance for the next eight months. After that it gradually retrenches for the next celebration.

Sometimes I love it, sometimes it fills me with irritation. Sometimes I try, by pruning, to improve its appearance; at others I leave it alone. After the hard winter of 1985 I couldn't wait to lop it all over and I felt a lot better. As far as the plant was concerned I should undoubtedly have acted more wisely by leaving it another three or four months and then approaching it cautiously, nibbling at its circumference rather than weighing in. The escallonia responded to my cavalier treatment by breaking into growth from all the old wood; then, as so often happens with evergreens, it went into reverse. Large sections died, others went on forging ahead. A question mark hangs over it. I might lose the entire shrub yet and I might not be too sad if I did. We cannot endlessly wait for Dame Nature in her infinite wisdom to

Clematis × jackmanii 'Superba' in the Long Border with the cut-leaved golden elder,
Sambucus racemosa 'Plumosa Aurea', which is pruned hard each winter,
and the shade-tolerant yellow daisy, *Telekia speciosa* (*Buphthalmum speciosum*).

guide us along the paths we should tread. Sometimes she needs a hefty kick in the buttocks. The subject is still wide open but will soon be resolved, I fancy.

The border's most splendid (and most photographed) feature comes into its own mid-month and lasts in beauty for some three weeks – quite a long time as these things go. It is the Mount Etna broom, *Genista aetnensis*, a fountain of tiny, yellow, scented blossom on a diaphanous framework that is virtually leafless. The effect is substantial and yet singularly light.

I planted Mount Etna in 1950, so it's a good age for a broom and is tree-like. But again, at planting, I never truly visualized its maturity. The neighbourhood area has been adapted as the situation has developed. Underneath its branches I have the 7-ft perennial *Inula magnifica*, whose yellow daisies have long, fine-spun rays and are out concurrently with the broom. The same colour, too, but rather a different plant.

To one side, *Clematis* × *jackmanii* 'Superba', which can usually be persuaded to climb into Mount Etna's branches, and that looks sumptuous. On the other side I have a pole specimen to 8 ft of the red rose 'Florence May Morse', which gives me two prolonged bouts of blossom, now and in the autumn. The flower shape is nothing special but the colour is crimson, without any pink or mauve mixed in, and there are all too few hardy border flowers of this straight red colouring. 'Florence May Morse' is normally expected to grow a mere 4 ft tall, so at double the height mine is something of a curiosity. It turned up mysteriously, some fifteen or twenty years ago, on our compost heap and must, I think, have sported from the bush form which I have in the Rose Garden.

Behind the rose is a privet, *Ligustrum* × *vicaryi*, with fairly large, lime green leaves and an abundance of white blossom.

Quite a pleasing herbaceous grouping in front of the broom and within its partial shade and that caused by the mulberry on the other side of the path: *Hosta ventricosa* 'Aureomarginata' ('Variegata') carries, in most years, a dense array of its 2-ft racemes of deep mauve bells. Behind it the pale yellow large-flowered day lily, *Hemerocallis* 'Marion Vaughan' (it really needs dead-heading every day), and intermingled with that, the 4-ft wild prototype, *Phlox paniculata* (from Margery Fish), with small mauve flowers. In the gloomier depths of the border here, I have more yellow daisies, *Telekia speciosa* (*Buphthalmum speciosum*), which self-sows; and the cut-leaved golden elder, *Sambucus racemosa* 'Plumosa Aurea'.

At the height of its season a border needs large, solid blocks of colour from perennial plants. On my heavy soil these are most naturally provided by border phloxes, which are at their best this month and the first half of next. The flower heads are a good, domed shape and they smell delicious. I don't mind, and in most cases don't know, what their names are, so long as they are strong and healthy. Most came from friends' gardens.

I have a tallish but self-supporting mauve phlox that has been in the garden longer than I have. Behind that the deep indigo monkshood, *Aconitum* 'Sparks's Variety', and in front I used to grow the invaluable crimson red *Monarda* 'Cambridge Scarlet'. This, alas, no longer likes me, not only having

The Lutyens-designed seat at the top of the Long Border,
with *Alchemilla mollis* and *Viola cornuta* 'Alba' prominent at the border front.

become a martyr to mildew but largely dying out each winter, so I am trying out substitutes: currently, *Penstemon* 'Drinkstone Red'. Left of this, *Campanula lactiflora* 'Prichard's Variety', which is 4 ft tall and a good deep mauve, though there are taller, paler, self-sown *lactiflora* seedlings nearby. Also a patch of white-flowered *Clematis recta*, which reaches 6 ft when properly supported, and this goes up into a pole honeysuckle, *Lonicera* × *americana*, which is pink and cream, the flowers borne in sprays. An excellent plant; scented, though not as much as some.

These plantings form the foreground to the most popularly photographed view at Dixter, with the house in the background. I like the plantings at the top of the border (where Lutyens's seat forms the end point) just as well if not better, but they have to be accepted for themselves, with only yews behind, though that is surely background enough for any gardener.

I have a weakness for yellow daisies, of which so many flower now and later. Here, at the back of the border, grows another tall one, *Ligularia doria*, and it is entirely self-supporting. People make a great fuss about plants being over-tall, yet their height gives them style and presence, qualities totally lacking in the plant breeders' pygmy triumphs that clamour around us at ankle height. Not being a pygmy myself, I have a natural preference for plants that I can see in detail without first lying down (I'm not too proud to lie on my belly in time of need, but the posture takes up a lot of ground space).

This ligularia resembles a giant yellow ragwort except that its dark green leaves, which have a rather sulky sheen, are smooth and quite undivided. It grows next to another *Clematis × jackmanii* 'Superba', this one trained up a pole as a vertical column. Purple and gold again. In front is a bush of the deepest purple-leaved *Cotinus coggygria*, and somewhere around here will be spires of the mullein *Verbascum chaixii*. The small yellow flowers have purple centres. It is a perennial but seeds itself and moves around, so I never quite know where it will be performing from year to year. When close to the cotinus, it looks particularly good and carefully planned. When close to the pink *Alstroemeria ligtu* hybrids near the border's front, the juxtaposition is more contentious. Nice visitors congratulate me on a daring combination. What the others say behind my back doesn't worry me too much.

There are large patches around here of mauve and pink phloxes, and the brashest pink one is also next to a forty-year-old Jerusalem sage, *Phlomis fruticosa*, whose whorls of hooded flowers are yellow. It is a fairly dusky shade but not pale, and I take no pride in the coupling. The sage is already out in June, before the phlox. As soon as it can decently be done, I dead-head it, or get someone else to do this unpopular job. It is an incredibly dusty shrub and brings on appalling hay fever, the sort that grips you in the throat and chest so that you can scarcely breathe. The only solution is to do the job after rain or when the sprinkler has just been at play. Well worth a pair of wet legs.

The small, slow-growing tree (marked on the plan) on the corner of the border by the cross-path is *Gleditsia triacanthos* 'Elegantissima'. I fell for this when I saw a mature specimen on Jackman's old Woking nursery (since built over) one January day more than thirty years ago, and my plant is that old. If you take to a deciduous shrub or tree when its leaves are off, you may be pretty certain that it will have year-round appeal. This is not a flowering tree but grown simply for its shape (the slower a tree grows the more character it develops) and for its light, pinnate foliage. Wood pigeons have a nest in it.

Further up the border and beyond the alstroemerias is a fairly classic (i.e. obvious) contrast in colour and form between the bronze daisies of *Helenium*

A hot spot in the Long Border, with *Helenium* 'Moerheim Beauty',
Salvia nemorosa 'Superba' and *Lychnis chalcedonica*.

'Moerheim Beauty' and the purple spikes of *Salvia nemorosa* 'Superba', both at $3\frac{1}{2}$ ft. The salvia requires some support but it is a stayer, producing a second flush of blossom in September. It gives better value than any of the more modern, dwarfer clones. Likewise the helenium. Its flowers are less well shaped than more modern cultivars, but if sympathetically dead-headed there'll be a worthwhile second crop to follow.

Behind the purple of the salvia are scarlet domes of *Lychnis chalcedonica*, which are excellent while they last, and there are no quarrelsome pink flowers near them at the time of their flowering, though there'll be hydrangeas and summer tamarisk later on.

If we now take a look at the border's central stretch, this is dominated by the vertical plumes of Dickson's golden elm (rather troublesome in the way its stock suckers) and of the pale grey willow, *Salix alba* 'Argentea'. In front of them is a patch of pale blue veronica (I'm not sure which one) whose height I restrain to 3 ft by resetting the clumps every March. Then a greeny-purple-leaved smoke bush, *Cotinus coggygria*, possibly 'Foliis Purpureis'; it is one of the best for developing a purple haze as the inflorescence continues to enlarge and expand after flowering, and this happens in July.

So a good deal is grown for foliage effect in this part of the border, where I also have a very old specimen of *Weigela florida* 'Variegata' and that makes a good background for (in some years) the pale yellow daisies of *Anthemis tinctoria* 'Wargrave', which I like to treat as an annual, planting newly rooted cuttings in the spring. By this method the plants flower non-stop from July to autumn and their height is conveniently restricted to 3 ft.

Another foliage specimen that is beginning to attain tree-like dimensions is the silver-variegated chestnut, *Castanea sativa* 'Albomarginata'. The white-margined leaves are reinforced at the end of the month by numerous clusters of cream-white male blossom. In front of it I grow an amazing foliage perennial, *Helianthus salicifolius*, which featured in the original border plan as *H. orgyalis*, though I do not remember it in those early days. Long, thin, arching leaves thickly clothe the stems which rise to 6 ft or more. It is never recognized as a sunflower at this stage, but looks like a cross between a lily and an Egyptian papyrus.

Near the front of the border I have a long wavy line of *Hydrangea serrata* 'Preziosa', the purplish colouring of whose young stems and leaves harmonizes with the purplish tints of *Allium christophii*, of which there is a lot hereabouts. This allium has unusually large, spherical heads on 1½-ft stems, and they hold their shape right through to autumn. After that they break off the stem and are bowled along by the wind until they get caught up in the fabric of some other plant. There they remain. In the following spring, a little clutch of thread-fine seedlings can be seen germinating underneath each old allium head. In this way, from a small original planting, I have *A. christophii* extensively. It's a good example of what a plant will do for you if you're not too busily tidy-minded. Something of the cottage garden mentality is an advantage. Neither must you cut down your border till the spring.

Similarly, around the skinny legs of a 'Chapeau de Napoléon' or 'Crested Moss' rose, there is a self-appointed colony of blue *Campanula persicifolia*. It looks just right with the old-fashioned pink of the rose. The latter is on its own roots, so that its suckers are its own. Originally it was a grafted plant that suckered briar understock. I layered one of its own long, whippy shoots, and when that was well established, dug out and gave away the parent!

Opposite above: After *Allium christophii* has faded, its colour and form
long persist, hovering above *Sedum* 'Ruby Glow', which has yet to flower.
Hydrangea serrata 'Preziosa' chimes in harmoniously.

Opposite below: Blue-stemmed sea holly, *Eryngium* × *oliverianum*,
hovering over *Diascia* 'Ruby Field' in the Long Border.

Above: The form of *Astilbe taquetii* contrasts well with the bun heads of *Hydrangea* 'Générale Vicomtesse de Vibraye' in the Barn Garden. *Arundinaria variegata* is in front.

Opposite: I have many hydrangeas in this part of the garden; here the dwarf red hortensia 'Westfalen' is in the foreground, with 'Blue Bird', a lacecap, behind.

I have a great partiality for hydrangeas, and they get going early in the month. It is supposed to be in good taste to *adore* all the lacecaps but to abhor those vulgar, mop-headed things, i.e. the hortensias. Well, I think that's a lot of self-conscious snob stuff. I love both kinds. Some are better than others and they can be more, or less, suitably sited; that's all.

Their season starts in early July. 'Générale Vicomtesse de Vibraye' is one of the earliest, but also one of the hardiest and the most persistently in flower. It keeps on developing more flower-bearing shoots. The colouring is light, and on my fairly neutral soil it comes pink. Where it grows, in the Barn Garden, it combines well with the mauve plumes of *Astilbe taquetii* 'Superba' (which sows itself true to type) and the dusky purplish foliage of *Rosa glauca* (*R. rubrifolia*). Also with the lavender blue cranesbill *Geranium pratense* 'Plenum Caeruleum'.

Another persistently flowering hortensia that gets early into its stride is the white 'Mme Emile Mouillère'. That grows in the Wall Garden (which suddenly becomes wide awake in July). If some of its earliest blossom grows tired looking and burnt half-way through the season, you have only to remove it and the display will continue even into early November, in a frost-free autumn. In front of 'Mme Mouillère' I have a large deep pink hortensia, 'Hamburg'. One plant of that to three of the white seems about the right balance.

The main hydrangea concentration is around the open-sided loggia between the house and the Topiary Garden. 'Bluebird', 'Blue Wave', 'Grayswood', 'Veitchii', 'Hidcote' and 'Geoffrey Chadbund' are some of the lacecaps I grow here, while the dwarfish, 3-ft 'Westfalen' is a notable red hortensia. Whatever their names may indicate, none of my hydrangeas is nearer to blue than lilac, but we have of late been dressing some of them with aluminium sulphate at fortnightly intervals from February to July, to see if a change to blue can be brought about. It is pretty slow, and if you do not immediately dissolve the salt crystals by watering them in, they scorch the foliage of other plants that have been touched. Neither have I yet found a cheap source for the chemical.

The climbing *Hydrangea petiolaris* flowered last month. Sorry you missed it but its season is short. This month we have, around my kitchen and larder windows, the even better *Schizophragma integrifolium*, with larger white, lozenge-shaped bracts. The only thing against this self-clinging climber is

Opposite: The lacecap hydrangea 'Geoffrey Chadbund' is a marvellous red on my neutral soil. This colour suits it better than the bluer tones produced by more acid soils.

Similar to the climbing hydrangea, but longer and later-flowering,
Schizophragma integrifolia has a more commanding presence but takes a number
of preliminary years to settle down to producing blossom.

that a plant seems (from the evidence that has reached me and certainly in my own case, though not mentioned in any book) to take at least ten years to settle down before it will start flowering. No use to those with itchy feet.

A curious tendril climber, which is flowering behind the main bedding-out area in front of the house, is *Mutisia oligodon*, with salmon pink daisy flowers. Against expectations, it seems to be reliably hardy under Sussex conditions. Indeed, there was for many years a plant in Crathes Castle Gardens in north-east Scotland. It vanished in the end but one wonders why.

In winter, when so few flowers are blooming, I and other garden authors will write in the greatest detail about witch hazels and winter sweets, snowdrops and the earliest irises. Nothing will escape our notice. But in the height of summer when so much is out and competing for our attention, it is difficult to do justice to it all. Indeed, some flowers will escape our attention altogether, and this is not just in the matter of describing them on paper. The sad fact is that plants may flower and fade before we have taken them in at all. Why bother to grow them, if that's our life style and we persist in being too

This is the tired businessman's flower, which waits till after four o'clock
in the afternoon before opening its yellow stars: *Asphodeline liburnica* intermixed
with the blue *Eryngium × oliverianum* in the Wall Garden.

preoccupied to look their way and register the pleasure of seeing them?
Rather than let this happen we should insist on taking enough time off from
the minutiae of daily affairs, so that we can live and share in the life of our
immediate surroundings. It is futile to let the best days of the year slip by with
nothing to recollect them by except the fact of having been too busy.

Even so, this book would become tedious if I paraded all my thousands of
plants, for this is a plantsman's garden. It has to be a 'highlights from . . .'
recording, leaving the complete picture for those with the stamina to come
and see for themselves, not once, but on repeated occasions.

I should like you, after four o'clock in the afternoon, to see the yellow-
starred asphodel, *Asphodeline liburnica*, which blooms in the evenings only. It
is in the Wall Garden. Behind it I had a big boskage formed by two
interlocked specimens of *Cistus × cyprius*, which is just about my favourite in
this none too hardy genus, of which I lost every plant in my garden in 1985.
But the replacements will not take too long to assert themselves. A fresh
crop of their large white discs with a maroon blotch at the base of each petal

opens every morning and shatters at midday. For this sort of flower it is worth being in the garden at six in the morning, to see the new flowers unfolding. Also, in reverse, to see the night's exhibition of evening primroses before they collapse. I have a pale yellow form of *Oenothera stricta* in a corner of the Wall Garden. It opens too late, as dusk gives way to night. Early morning is the time to enjoy it. Almost the whole animal kingdom, butterflies apart, seems to be up and busy at this hour at this season. Even the grass snakes are on their sunbathing pad long before the sun has reached them. And the air is alive with the sound of bees, though wild bees are far more matinal than their hive cousins.

Still in the Wall Garden, then, I have a good large-flowered strain of the tree mallow, *Lavatera olbia*, which is a variable plant – if I let it self-sow, the seedlings are always inferior. This is a fast-growing, short-lived shrub. If it survived the previous winter, its season will get under way early in July, the first blooms being the largest and most important, but a succession of their open mallow-mauve funnels will continue right into autumn.

Beside this, a clematis of tremendous vigour, *Clematis* × *jouiniana* 'Prae-cox'. It is a non-climber, so its trails are partly supported on a pole and partly allowed to ramble forwards to the border's margin. It carries a mass of tiny blue-white cruciform blossom from late July for a good two months.

In a fairly shady border I have a colony of *Veratrum album*, a hardy perennial within the *Liliaceae*, having a tremendous presence. At 5 ft its sturdy, upright stems explode into a branching panicle of white stars. Mauve hostas flower in front of and to the right of this – the one called 'Tall Boy', which has a long season.

Much of the garden is filled with the scent of honeysuckles at the early hour that I have been recommending for a first appreciation, but as the day warms up, *Philadelphus*, the mock oranges, are apt to take over and you find yourself moving from the orbit of one specimen to that of the next.

A scent of a different kind pervades the Barn Garden; that of the dragon arum, *Dracunculus vulgaris*, whose splendid purple arum flowers inveigle the attentions of their bluebottle pollinators by smelling of bad meat. I have this aroid in a moist and fairly shady border. The size of its flowers and their numbers greatly benefit if a colony is split and replanted fairly frequently.

Another notable in the Barn Garden is *Yucca gloriosa* 'Nobilis', which is less stiff than its prototype but no less imposing and a very free flowerer. The leaves have an elegant twist on them and there is a glaucous bloom on both surfaces. Like other yuccas this one may bloom at any time from June to November, but is most apt to do so now.

The white panicles of *Veratrum album* have great presence in a garden.
In front, *Hosta ventricosa* 'Variegata' (called 'Aureomarginata' in America),
which flowers freely. Veratrums are apt to have years of blindness.

The floor of the Sunk Garden is largely colonized by the creeping *Acaena novae-zelandiae* and, additionally and self-appointed, by birdsfoot trefoil, *Lotus corniculatus*. The young burrs on the acaena turn bright carmine now, while the trefoil is yellow. This is a surprisingly good mix. Our worst weed in the Sunk Garden is a creeping vetch, *Vicia sepia*, which mixes itself into everything. The only successful treatment, and it is successful, is to dab its young growth with glyphosate, which we buy as Roundup.

I like to see a vertical feature rising like a geyser's water column from the flat expanse of its surroundings. And so, in the Sunk Garden, I have removed a paving stone in order to accommodate the giant reed grass, *Arundo donax* (I also have it among my hydrangea colony on the other side of the house). It never flowers with me, but its leaves seem to have been carved out of blue steel. It loves moisture and warmth, and in a good season will rise within three or four months to 14 ft from scratch. It is hardy, but will not prosper in a cold climate.

Among several other ornamental grasses in the Barn Garden is *Calamagrostis acutiflora* 'Stricta', which needs, to set it off, an open site where it can stand well above all neighbours. It quickly reaches its full stature of 6 ft now, and the flowering stems are dead straight, like rods, and closely set. The flower panicles are dove mauve, fluffy at first but soon closing into upright rat's tails, which slowly change in colour to fawn and then bleach palest straw. The plant still has presence as I write, in February.

Another plant that I can recommend for a place where it is tallest among much lower neighbours is the wand flower, *Dierama pulcherrimum*. This has colonized, by self-sowing, our sitting-out terrace on the south-west side of the house. Its stems are strong yet flexible, so that they rise to 5 ft and then arch over under the weight of blossom, which consists of a series of pink or magenta funnels.

There are two self-sowers in the Barn Garden which are at the height of their powers and which go very well together, though you never know from year to year what the balance between them will be. One is the monocarpic *Eryngium giganteum*, known as Miss Willmott's ghost, of a stiff habit to 3 ft with a ruff of grey bracts surrounding a dome of sea-green blossom. The other is *Lychnis coronaria*, another 3-footer whose dazzling magenta moon flowers are perfectly set off by felted grey stems and leaves. They go well near the dusky pink and grey foliage of *Fuchsia magellanica* 'Versicolor'. Among all these, the annual grass, *Briza maxima*, has been flowering for the past month with its panicles of dangling, heart-shaped lockets. It will soon be over, and should be pulled out pretty smartly to prevent it seeding incontinently.

If you notice an escallonia on the east side of the Barn Garden, it is *Escallonia virgata*, a deciduous species with tiny leaves and short spikes of white stars. Very fresh. It has far greater style and quality than the cascade hybrids like 'Langleyensis' that have arisen from it. But the flowering season is a mere ten days.

Our long grass at this season gets some visitors extremely worried. All that worries me is when the inconsiderate trample it down. That does look bad. Photographers are apt to be the worst offenders. The professionals are usually very considerate about where they put their feet and their tripods; the amateurs less so.

Of flowers in the grass, the tufted vetch, *Vicia cracca*, is my favourite. It is a vigorous climbing herb with short, dense spikelets of rich lavender flowers. If it finds support, like a hedge, it makes a curtain of colour to 5 ft, but looks almost as good among grass stems and with the yellow pea and birdsfoot trefoil.

In damp places, and especially at the bottom of the Upper Moat, there is masses of cream-white meadow sweet. I have also established the pink meadow sweet, *Filipendula rubra* 'Venusta', near to the Horse Pond, where it is happy among the dogwoods. It has spread amazingly fast.

In the last week of the month, grass cutting begins. We start by hiring an Allenscythe for a few days and with it get into all the small, awkward patches, starting with the meadow areas in front of the house. I am chiefly concerned that the camassias should have ripened and spilt their seeds. It is always a close-run thing. The Allenscythe is followed, when the mowings have been carted and used to start a compost heap, by a wheel horse and sweep, getting the grass really tight. It always looks the colour of parchment at this stage, no matter how dry or wet the weather, but greens up within days.

Once the long grass has gone it is a relief to be without it for another season, but the whole business of cutting and carrying and of trimming difficult places takes us well into September.

The old globe artichoke bed is cropping as hard as it knows how this month, and I cut them practically every day – the hearts if not the whole head, when there's pressure of supplies. But this is an extremely social month – all your urban friends like to come and tell you how lucky you are to live in the country (they're not so keen in the slushy season). Everyone likes, or quickly comes to like, artichokes, even the children. They tend to be more conservative than adults about food, but can't resist the petal-peeling ritual.

The summer raspberry, 'Delight', is in now; a huge, wet fruit, hopeless in bad weather but most gratifyingly quick to pick when it is dry. It takes very few berries to fill a bowl. There are currants, black and red, to deal with and the gooseberries keep on.

Because of our congenitally late sowings we shall still not have many vegetables, but there'll be quantities of 'Little Gem' lettuce. They hold well and few will be wasted. I have yet to meet a better lettuce than this. I liked the old name 'Sugar Cos', which suited it.

August

T HE post-harvest countryside of August looks bleached and dusty, while the trees are heavy. They have lost the freshness of early summer, while the glow of autumn has not yet arrived. The oaks sometimes flush a second crop of young foliage in July, but this almost immediately goes down to mildew.

A garden in August should be an oasis and, given cooperation from the weather, mine is that and a pleasant place to be in. Many foliage plants are all the while becoming increasingly lush and there is plenty of flower colour, although a falling off inevitably sets in from the middle of the month. It is the hardy perennials which falter, but that can be largely compensated for by annuals and bedding plants.

When fine and warm, with heavy morning dews, August is summer still and I find it easy to persuade myself that it will go on like this for ever, in a kind of timeless state of suspension. It is lovely to be able to walk into the garden in the early morning without needing to don even a light dressing-gown and to feel perfectly relaxed and warm.

Most of the birds are silent, while they moult (the cock blackbirds, with bald patches around their eyes, look particularly disreputable and cross), but there are exceptions. Sparrows keep up their monotonous cheeping; the collar doves their no less tedious morse code long-short-long, alternated with a strangled peacock wail when flying between perches. Very much on the plus side, we have the swallows, still as vocally cheerful as ever and as sleek of plumage. With their hordes of young becoming ever stronger on the wing, they have built up to large populations and are joined by house martins from elsewhere (they have not nested with us for many years), sunning themselves and preening on the roofs or performing a roundelay as they wheel and dip over the Horse Pond.

But at six in the morning I most like, perhaps in order to start the sprinkler, to visit the Barn Garden. Enclosed and private, it has an intimate feel. When I

Opposite: Part of the Horse Pond in mid August, with waterlily 'Rose Arey'.
Spikes of self-sown purple loosestrife grow on the near bank.

say 'come on' to Tulip, burrowing under hosta leaves, it's like speaking in a well-furnished room. But the *Eucryphia* 'Nymansay' is already like a work-shop, so thick with bees collecting nectar. The eucryphia buds push off their nightcaps (poppy style) and then rapidly expand, like a newly emerged butterfly drying its wings. There is a mass of stamens in the centre of each white flower and the tiny pinpoint anthers are red.

The next shrub to this is *Hydrangea villosa*, the best thing in the August garden. The bees are all over this too, but a little later, when the pollen has dried, for this is what they are collecting and you can tell it from the blue pollen sacs that build up on their legs. The hydrangea's fertile flowers are blue but the showier sterile blooms are rich lilac.

Another bush on which the bees are foraging from an early hour is the myrtle, *Myrtus communis*, on the terrace. I like to open and keep open the garden door that leads on to this terrace from the moment I get up, so that the myrtle's spicy scent can be drawn into and waft through the house. Another scent that is currently channelled in is the summer jasmine's, *Jasminum officinale* 'Affine'. Because, of course, we plant for scents where we sit out.

This terrace faces south-west and is protected by house shadow from the full blaze of the sun until two o'clock in the afternoon, so it is the best spot to enjoy pre-prandial drinks (and I confess to being particularly fond of champagne, in the morning, when I have friends to enjoy it with).

Four large ornamental pots stand out here. In hot weather I water them with a gallon a day, quickly upturned from a can or bucket which I can fill from the nearby pantry. Once or twice a week I add a feed of Phostrogen.

These pots are mainly planted with ivy-leaved 'geraniums', of which 'Ville de Paris' alias 'King of the Balkans' is one of my favourites. It has small salmon flowers, but I also have a red-flowered strain of the same variety. I cannot say that I like one more than the other. You see this pelargonium everywhere on the Continent and yet it has never become out-and-out popular here. By contrast, *Helichrysum petiolatum* and *H. microphyllum* are appreciated as tub and window-box grey foliage plants with us, but little on the Continent. It is the small-leaved *H. microphyllum* that I use on the terrace. Also the trailing blue *Convolvulus mauritanicus*, which flowers non-stop from early June to late autumn. The funnel flowers are almost (not quite) pure blue on expanding in the morning. It is curious to notice how they are recessed with straight lines at an angle to the line of the funnel. Around four in the afternoon they fade to mauve and gradually close.

My other ornamental pots are in and around the Sunk Garden. The pond provides a quick dip water supply. There are two stone seats on opposite

Helichrysum petiolatum, a grey-leaved, tender perennial, is a most accommodating and flexible plant for lapping over the hard edge of pots and other display containers. Here it is seen with the 'geranium' 'Maxim Kovaleski' in the Sunk Garden.

sides of this garden and so, for the early part of the season, I plant some mignonette in the pots here, and heliotrope for later; a 'geranium' for colour and the felted heart-leaved *Helichrysum petiolatum* to break the line of the pot margin and spread outwards far beyond it. But in the single pot in the floor of the Sunk Garden I train a shoot of a centrally placed helichrysum up a cane, clipping it in to its support as it grows. It then branches horizontally and makes a little tree. John Treasure gave me this tip; I don't know if he discovered it himself. With this helichrysum I usually have a couple of *Cuphea cyanea* plants, with orange, tubular flowers that are all the more brightly coloured for the plants being confined at the root; and the blue daisies of *Felicia amelloides* 'Santa Anita'. But of course it's nice to change things a little from year to year.

I used to have koi carp (which I bought at Harrods as tiddlers) in the Sunk Garden pond, and I fed them morning and evening from April to October.

They were voracious. But they bred far too freely. Also, carp are burrowing fish. They constantly disturbed the water. It was always turbid and green. You couldn't even see the fish except when they were taking trout pellets at the surface. Eventually I got a friend in the pond business to take them all away for me – there must have been nearly 200 of them. Since then I've got on so well without any fish – there are wild newts, after all – and the water has been so pleasantly clear, even in early summer, that I have resisted starting again. As an underwater oxygenator I have put in some rosettes of the water soldier, *Stratiotes aloides*. The water was too disturbed for this to establish when the carp were there, but it is happy now and I like the subaqueous patterns that it makes.

I have written nothing yet about the annuals I bed out into the garden for the summer. Several other months besides August depend quite heavily on them, but different batches come into their own at different times.

The main bedding-out area is in front of the house. There are subsidiary patches in a number of other small beds, and I also work some into the Long Border, while the lupins that I generally grow in the High Garden are followed by late-sown annuals. Latest of all will be the follow-on to a display of sweet williams, which is a flower I come back to at frequent intervals. It cannot be scrapped until the end of July.

I like the excuse to grow plenty of annuals, because I love their freshness. Those that flower most intensively from August onwards are especially rewarding, because there are fewer hardy perennials contributing. Annuals give me ample opportunities to experiment. Every year I'm doing something different with them, so they cannot be written about as though they were constants. It saddens me that so many visitors lose interest in those they admire on hearing that they *are* annuals. The majority that I grow must, indeed, be raised by the garden's owner, as they will never be found in garden centres. Even the marigolds (*Tagetes*) that I go in for will not be the kinds seen with any frequency in garden centres. They like a compact, early-maturing strain that starts flowering before it is sold. I like one that makes a good large plant before it thinks about flowering. Marigolds have the great advantage that they can be moved successfully when they are already large plants. So I can line my plants out until there's a place ready to receive them – perhaps after sweet williams or *Verbascum olympicum* – and then move them in already coming into flower and big enough as plants to be spaced at 2 ft.

Opposite: This year I used the stately biennial *Verbascum olympicum* in narrow borders which can be seen across the topiary lawn from a Lutyens garden seat.

The blue-leaved *Melianthus major* is just about my favourite foliage plant.
Crowns should be protected in winter with peat or bracken. The purple, plain-leaved
Perilla adjoining is an annual, but, worse luck, no longer in commerce.

I do this sort of thing with chrysanthemums, too, either using named varieties or raising plants of one or other of the early-maturing seed strains that are available these days. The plants require a heavy watering both before and after their move, so it is quite heavy and exacting work but rewarding.

There are various ways in which mixed borders can be kept lively at this time. One is by the use of good foliage. *Melianthus major* is just about the most beautiful foliage plant that you can grow outside – or you can bed it out if you do not trust it to survive the winter. Its large smooth pinnate leaves are sea-green and strongly toothed at the margins. When the edge of one leaf casts its shadow on its neighbour, as happens when the light is low, it looks amazingly three-dimensional.

This contrasts well with canna foliage. Cannas have broad, spathulate leaves. I have one that is purple-flushed, known as *Canna indica* 'Purpurea'. *C. iridiflora* has a broad green leaf and arching racemes of pink flowers. *C. musaefolia* is a recent acquisition from Holland, with particularly handsome, banana-like leaves, flushed purple. Seedlings of *Geranium maderense* are good value as foliage plants. They grow quickly and the palmate leaves radiating from a woody central crown are extremely handsome. *Fatsia japonica* is a stalwart among the hardy shrubs, but it never stops shedding old leaves the summer through. Carrying armfuls of these off the scene is an unceasing task.

Ferns are a great standby in shadier places (though many of them are in sunshine), while the ornamental grasses liven up sunnier positions. The pale elegance of *Miscanthus sinensis* 'Variegatus' is notable. It goes well with the purple heads of the excellent *Verbena bonariensis*, which I have in many parts of the garden. It self-sows and has a tremendously long season, being by now some 5 ft tall. It is never an obstructive plant, as you can see through its stems, so it can often be allowed to grow up at the border's front.

Left: *Crocosmia masonorum* 'Dixter Flame' is of my own breeding, and is seen here at the top of the Long Border through *Verbena bonariensis* and backed by *Tamarix ramosissima* (*T. pentandra*), which I cut hard back each winter.

Right: *Verbena bonariensis*, visited by a Painted Lady butterfly, is backed by *Miscanthus sinensis* 'Variegatus'. The verbena self-sows in many parts of the garden, flowering from July to November.

Hydrangea × *macrophylla* 'Ayesha' has a long season. It is peculiar in that its florets incurve and they are glazed like porcelain. It needs a sheltered position.

At the top of the Long Border, for instance, I have it among and above a red clone of *Crocosmia masonorum* that I call 'Dixter Flame'. It is my own seedling. In the High Garden I like the verbena near to the deep pink mallow, *Malope trifida*, with which I sometimes replace the lupins. Together with teasels, the verbena also sows itself in the Rose Garden and makes a welcome change in plant form to rose bushes. It is popular with butterflies, and if there is a hatch of Painted Ladies, while the verbena is in flower, it is sure to be visited by them.

The summer tamarisk, *Tamarix ramosissima* (*T. pentandra*), is just what you need in a border from now on. Its tiny pale green leaves are airy, and especially striking after a dewy night. Branch by branch the shrub will open

Three levels at the top of the Long Border. The cardoon, *Cynara cardunculus*, behind; white spikes of moisture-loving *Cimifuga ramosa*, centre; *Hydrangea* 'Mariesii' in front.

its innumerable spikelets of pink blossom over the next six weeks. Following a hard winter pruning it flowers on the young wood at 6 ft and again goes well with *Verbena bonariensis*. A firmer associate in this context (we are at the top of the Long Border) is *Hydrangea* 'Mariesii', with flat heads of pink flowers that are not quite lacecap, as there are large florets at the centre of the corymb as well as at the margin.

I grow *H.* × *macrophylla* 'Ayesha' near to a wall in the Barn Garden, since it has a reputation for tenderness. This striking cultivar, which is light pink on my soil, has domed heads of incurved florets that are so glazed as to resemble porcelain. Its season lasts from July to November, as it is continually developing new flower heads.

On the other, sunny, side of its wall I have *Cestrum parqui*, with panicles of light green flowers. By day they have a funny little sour smell, but quite late in the evening they suddenly start to exhale a powerfully sweet fragrance with a kind of nutty flavour in it. If you're never in the right spot when this happens, as is my fate, bring two or three panicles indoors as captive performers.

Among the freshest flowers of August and September are the varieties of *Hydrangea paniculata* called 'Tardiva' and 'Floribunda'. They flower on the young wood, and the harder you prune them in winter, the larger the resulting flower heads. I don't overdo this myself, and they flower for me at about 5–6 ft with panicles of cream-white blossom wherein the tiny fertile florets are mixed in with the big showy ones.

In a large border, the cardoon, *Cynara cardunculus*, is a dual-purpose plant. Early on its great, grey acanthus leaves are magnificent. Then the flowering stems gradually take over, opening into blue, artichoke-like candelabra in August *(p. 137)*. It's a nuisance in demanding the very securest support.

I am grateful to *Artemisia lactiflora* for flowering at 6 ft and yet being entirely self-supporting. Its creamy panicles have quite a long season of beauty, and can be considerably enlivened if a few nonchalant strands of red nasturtium can be persuaded to wander over them. I also like these with my featherbed of *Aster sedifolius* (*A. acris*), which is an August flower, lavender blue, and requiring plentiful support from peasticks.

I have a splendid August-flowering torch lily in *Kniphofia uvaria* 'Nobilis', 7 ft tall and with large orange flares. *Artemisia lactiflora* goes well with that.

A pretty combination at the front of the Long Border at its top end is made by the poly-pom rose 'The Fairy', which has shiny leaves and panicles of small, clear pink double flowers, with Chinese chives, *Allium tuberosum*, 18 inches tall with heads of white, green-centred flowers. It sows itself.

I used to enjoy *Sedum* 'Ruby Glow' in August beneath my principal *Allium christophii* colony, but it has been attacked at the root by vine weevil larvae (those horrid, pudgy little white grubs) and by a web-forming caterpillar (a tortrix moth, I suspect) on its foliage. But *Sedum spectabile* has been with us since the beginning of time and never fails. Typically this is an almost too pale pink, so that I prefer the more definitely shaded 'Brilliant'. The latter is always sporting back to the pale prototype, and actually a mixture of both shades is prettiest of all. This is the plant that butterflies flock to, not to 'Autumn Joy', which is just starting its long season.

If you want your borders to go on looking presentable till the end of the year, and I most certainly do want that, they need constant small attentions.

A view of Dixter from the east across the 'conversation piece' of topiary birds.
Reserves of perennials (*Echinacea purpurea* in the foreground) are grown in this area.

Weedings, obviously, but more than that. So many plants require tidying up
after they have flowered, and tidying in the way that will suit them best.

Alchemilla mollis develops a brown, trodden-on look from the end of July,
and anyway needs to be prevented from self-seeding. I like to cut the plants
right back to the crown all over so that no leaf remains. New foliage will
appear shortly. The alternative is to pull out the flowered stems, which break
off cleanly and easily at the base, and that will leave a furnishing of old foliage
that doesn't look too bad and certainly less initially bald than following the
first method.

I quite often cut the early-flowering *Hemerocallis flava* right down, as its old
leaves become pretty sordid. It soon grows new foliage and will sometimes
carry a few blooms in the autumn, doubtless at the expense of next year's
crop, but that will not be noticed.

Border phloxes need dead-heading, back to the first pair of leaves below
the panicle. I hate to see an inch of stalk left above these leaves. The earliest-

flowering kinds will quite often carry a worthwhile second crop, especially if the colony is young and luxuriant and the summer warm.

The great thing is to look at the border critically, and the best time to notice what wants doing is when you're showing it to a visitor. Lapses in upkeep can seem mortifyingly noticeable then.

Even if August makes its exit in a blaze of heat, the feeling of autumn will have crept in at some stage in the month and I like that. The sun mellows and there is a decreasing tendency to harshness in the midday light. This is kinder to flowers and is nowhere more noticeable than in the second big flush from repeat-flowering roses, which gets going in the last half of the month. Their colours, especially of buff-orange roses like 'William Allen Richardson', 'Buff Beauty', 'Chanel' and 'Silva', are more intense. The magenta of 'Mme Isaac Pereire' is richer, deeper. Some of them, like 'The Fairy', which hovers over a glaucous mat of *Acaena affinis*, start up only in mid-July but run on continuously for the rest of the season.

Our principal task of getting meadow areas cut and neat once more continues throughout the month, but even before it has been completed we need to give a second close cropping to the meadow in front of the house where there are colchicums. They start flowering in the last week and they'll overlap with crocuses in September. This is our last chance until the final cut of the year in November. All mowings are removed to the compost heap. I dislike picking them up on my feet, still worse on my clothes when I'm reclining on the ground, which I constantly am near the Horse Pond, where so much is always going on. Lots of paying visitors enjoy lying on the grass, too. It seems to be an English habit. I never noticed anyone doing it in Germany.

At last there is an abundance of fresh vegetables to draw on from our all too late sowings. But they are welcome now, as I have family and house guests and some of them don't mind helping to prepare the vegetables as well as eat them. Not that I mind preparing them myself; in fact I really enjoy shucking peas that haven't become too fat in their pods. Broad beans sown in bulk at the end of April will mostly go into the deep freeze. Shucking these is an untidy job. I think the best policy is to pare away the ridge on one (either) side of the pod with a knife so that it opens out without trying to twist itself into a spiral.

Time was when we grew masses of plums. Bird bud-pecking problems have made this impossible, alas, so I buy quantities of near-ripe 'Early Rivers', early in the month. It is a free-stoning black plum and by far the tastiest both for freezing and for jam making – the stones having been first extracted. We used to grow half a dozen trees of this variety and they had the common habit of biennial bearing. The finest of them, which grew near to the Rose Garden where I now have a double red hawthorn, was tremendously laden in its last year, and I failed to take the weight off its branches by propping each of them up on a forked stick, or strod, in Sussex dialect. Came a sudden shower and the whole lot broke. There was nothing left of the tree but its trunk.

In the fourth week of August we may hope to start eating a fig crop if it is one of the lucky years for this fruit. Even then it has to be worked for. Figs have many admirers – rats, squirrels, wasps, starlings and blackbirds. Time-consuming ladder work is necessary, and not many figs can be reached from one ladder position. My method is to fix a lettuce bag over each fig, securing it to the branch behind with a wire stem tie. That's done just as the fruit begins to colour. Three or four days later it will be dead ripe, with longitudinal skin splits. A bag-removing and refixing operation is repeated. So long as there are plenty of figs to play with, the trouble is infinitely rewarded.

A late August task which may even need a memory-jogging diary entry is to sow certain annual seeds that benefit from a long growing period. It's too early yet for cornflowers – they'll just run prematurely to flower – and I wouldn't trust *Cynoglossum amabile* yet either, but sweet scabious, *Scabiosa atropurpurea*, goes in, and viscaria, which is really a lychnis. The strain called 'Rose Angel' makes a vivid display in June and is short enough, at 1 ft, not to need support. Some I'll raise now to bed out in early spring; others to grow in pots for display outside the porch. *Dianthus* F1 'Queen of Hearts' should be sown, too, and 'Rainbow Loveliness', if I have not already done so in July. I'm always glad to have a patch of this opening its scented flowers in June. Its seed ripens quickly enough to be sown immediately, for next year's display.

Then I must not forget to repot my *Gladiolus tristis* corms. If they have been kept bone dry in their old pots at the back of the greenhouse bench, which is the best treatment, they'll still be dormant. But as soon as potted I water them and place the pots outside, where they will receive further waterings, and they break swiftly into new growth.

September

———————————◆———————————

THERE is no need to bewail the declining year. Autumn is a glorious season in its own right, and as pleasant as summer to spend in the garden. The weather has to remain kind for this to come true, but the same can be said of any month or season.

There is a probability that we shall encounter strong winds at some stage. Equinoctial gales are not just in the imagination. That said, I have noticed that this does not yet spell the end of the garden. A gale in September may leave sad, tattered remnants in its wake, but if the weather mends, the garden still retains enough resilience itself to mend.

On fine Thursday mornings I'm back on the stone seat in the Sunk Garden to write my weekly piece for *Country Life*. I have to bring with me one dog's bed (for Tulipa), one thick cushion (for me), a writing board and pad and any works of reference I think I may need (none, if I can help it).

At the near edge of the pond in front of me is a plant of *Iris laevigata* 'Zambesi'. It has deep blue flowers. The strange thing about it is that instead of having an obvious flowering season, say June, when it's all in bloom, like other conventional irises, followed by eleven months when there are no flowers, this one puts up two flowering stems in June, another couple in July and so on right into November. This is companionable in it and I appreciate its company.

However, there'll always be a sprinkling of visitors who can depress me about my garden, who can't see any colour left in it but who can see the weeds; forgetting them, I think my garden's rather good in September. I'm more surprised at how much there is flowering rather than how little, and that feeling often persists through October, always depending on the weather's cooperation. The fact is I love autumn as a season, and if you like a season well enough you automatically find yourself taking steps to surround yourself with good things that will bolster up the image.

Opposite: September is the easiest month in which to flower *Lilium formosanum*. Its night scent is delicious. From seed to first flower takes only six to eight months, but the display here is in the second year.

When I took this picture, on 23 September,
it was still too early in the morning for butterflies to be on the wing.
A little later, *Escallonia bifida* puts any buddleia to shame.
Alas, it is none too hardy and needs a very sheltered, sunny wall.

There has usually been a new hatch of various butterflies to help things along. Having been saying for most of the summer that it's been a bad year for them, suddenly it doesn't seem so bad after all. Besides the usual Tortoiseshells and the year's recent hatch of Peacocks, there'll usually be quite a few Commas and Common Blues, perhaps some Holly Blues, Brimstones, Speckled Woods in the shadier parts of the garden and, if it was a good migrating year, Painted Ladies and Red Admirals. These last have a preference for rotting fruit, especially pears, and with luck there'll be 'William's' pears to pick early in the month (leaving plenty of windfalls) and 'Comice' at the end. The other butterflies mostly find their nectar from daisy

With *Schizophragma* and the climbing hydrangea, *Pileostegia viburnoides* makes up a triumvirate of related, self-clinging, white-flowered climbers. It is last to flower, and is evergreen. Note the late-flowering privet, *Ligustrum quihoui*, top left; the hydrangeas 'Mme Emile Mouillière (white) and 'Hamburg' in front.

flowers, of which I have masses, but also from *Verbena bonariensis*, which goes from strength to strength, from late-flowering buddleias, and, most startlingly, because they show up so brilliantly on its white blossom, from *Escallonia bifida*.

This is my favourite species by far. It is like *E.* × 'Iveyi', but better. The scented flowers are star-shaped, without tubes, and they are gathered into big panicles. September is their month. Alas that this species should be rather tender, but it deserves the warmest wall you can offer.

Another shrub the butterflies adore is *Clerodendrum bungei*, which belongs to the verbena family. Above large, dark green heart leaves it carries domed corymbs of deep carmine buds which open to scented flowers. They can be savoured at a considerable distance. This is a suckering shrub. Sometimes its suckers come up where I could never have deliberately planted anything, and I am grateful. At others they come through another plant and threaten its extinction. *C. bungei* will tolerate a lot of shade. If cut to the ground by winter frost, it comes too late into flower the next autumn, but if most of this growth is spared, September is its high spot. That grows in the Wall Garden, except where it has strayed through the brick archway.

There's a good grouping now in a moderately shaded corner on the other side of *Fatsia japonica*. With panicles of tiny white blossom, *Ligustrum quihoui* is in full flower – 12 ft or more tall and with neat foliage. It is an elegant species. Against the wall to its right there is a froth of creamy white from the self-clinging evergreen climber, *Pileostegia viburnoides (p. 145)*. In front, *Hydrangea × macrophylla* 'Mme Emile Mouillère' is still doing her stuff and merely needs dead-heading. There are pink Japanese anemones on her left, white *Allium tuberosum* in front and, next to that, the dainty mauve funnels of *Hosta lancifolia*. Here, then, is a typical mixed border community.

At the other end of the Wall Garden, where it is sunniest, I always like the twinning of *Fuchsia* 'Mrs Popple' in front and *Abelia × grandiflora* behind. The fuchsia is rather heavyweight, having sombre green foliage, but does a job in suppressing an ineradicable weed, *Oxalis rubra*. 'Mrs Popple' is red and purple, 3 ft or more tall, and flowers most freely in autumn. The abelia grows up to 6 ft and carries small, off-white funnel flowers non-stop for several months. They are backed by a persistent pinkish calyx, which is a feature in itself.

Fuchsias are pretty good in September and often even better next month, if frost holds off as it usually does at Dixter. On the Long Border I have *Fuchsia magellanica* 'Riccartonii', not in the border itself but on the opposite, orchard side where it colonizes the start of a piece of dry walling. You can never be certain when it will be at its best, but September is a fairly safe bet and it is a popular flower with bees.

The red-and-yellow lanterns with protruding brown stamens of *Abutilon megapotamicum* have a long season, but it varies dramatically from year to year according to the severity of the previous winter. In any case this has its best chance against a wall in the warmest corner of the Barn Garden. Nearby I have a somewhat tender sub-shrub, *Eupatorium ligustrinum*, with corymbs of white tubular flowers. This attracts butterflies. I should also mention the herbaceous *E. rugosum*, white flowered at 3 ft and usefully late. It self-sows and sometimes does it unexpectedly well, as on top of a wall.

I think my favourite *Cimicifuga* is *C. ramosa*, which grows to 6 ft at the top of the Long Border, but Beth Chatto has given me the even more exciting purple-leaved, purple-stemmed *C.r.* 'Atropurpurea', which shows off the spires of white blossom to perfection. Nurserymen take short cuts when they can and some of them are raising this from seed, instead of by the slow process of division. Seedlings vary greatly in the amount of purple pigment in their foliage. Your nurseryman will tell you that he throws out the green-leaved ones, but some pretty greenish stuff gets through his net and should have no claim to the title 'Atropurpurea' (black-purple).

Anemones belong to the same family. Their similar foliage is the give-away. I grow lots of single white Japanese anemones behind my chief bedding-out area in front of the house. What lovelier flower is there than this? The green eye and yellow stamens give it just the right enlivening touch. With these anemones I have two clumps of the white-variegated dogwood, *Cornus alba* 'Elegantissima', and, when I can grow them, some bushes of grey *Artemisia arborescens*. However, their foliage is constantly plagued by house sparrows and even black-cottoning is not always successful in saving them.

In front of the anemones there must be some bedding display that is currently at its peak. I've been rather inclined to white or yellow flowers here,

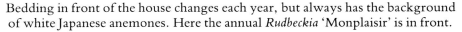

Bedding in front of the house changes each year, but always has the background of white Japanese anemones. Here the annual *Rudbeckia* 'Monplaisir' is in front.

of recent years. White begonias or busy lizzies, for instance, or yellow annual rudbeckias. Whatever it is doesn't want to be too tall, otherwise the anemones look walled in.

Outside my larder and in other cool places there are willow gentians, *Gentiana asclepiadea*; arcs of deep blue funnels. They have pleasant self-sowing habits, even into a lawn, though that has to be unsuccessful. They go well with ferns and hostas. The late hosta for this month is 'Royal Standard', with fresh green foliage and scented white funnels, inherited from *Hosta plantaginea*. Colonies deteriorate quite quickly if they are not frequently split and re-set. 'Honeybells' is so bad in this respect, and also liable to bud drop if the soil is at all dry at flowering, that I have cast it out.

I keep telling myself that I must *do* something with *Schizostylis coccinea* 'Major' instead of merely selling it from a nursery row. It is one of the earliest of its tribe in flower and so doesn't have to be considered as an unacceptable passenger in a long run-up. Its spikes of bowl-shaped red flowers cover a long season. It should look good with the blue of one of the hardy plumbagos. *Ceratostigma willmottianum* is the brighter colour but the tenderer plant. *C. plumbaginoides* is a darker, sulkier blue, but its foliage can be relied upon to flare up brightly later on.

There is something special about *Kirengeshoma palmata* that you do not meet in many herbaceous perennials; the dark stems, the unusual cut of its maple-like leaves, and then the drooping clusters of its pale yellow shuttle-cock flowers, which open from fat buds. I saw them looking so good in a Dutch garden, behind the scarlet-berried clubs of *Arum italicum* 'Pictum', that I have imitated this planting in a shady border.

Although I am not yet using it as effectively as I should (but that will come), I must again put in a word of praise for the fresh green and white foliage of the comfrey, *Symphitum* × *uplandicum* 'Variegatum', which is so much more luxuriant in the flush that follows flowering and after you have cut the plant down. Another foliage plant that is at its most prosperous-looking now is *Kniphofia caulescens*, with its glaucous straps. This is a plant that needs presenting. In paving or in a gravel sweep is ideal but I have it on the right-angled corner of a border, and that's not too bad. It flowers in September, for what that's worth. Not much with me. The flower buds usually rot or half rot in the crown, just as they are developing.

Berberis thunbergii 'Gold Ring' is mainly for foliage, though pretty, also, when flowering in the spring. The narrow green margin around each leaf only develops in maturity, and it gives point to the whole shrub in a way that a plain leaf cannot do. It has a long season of heightened colour in the fall.

Asclepias tuberosa, known as butterfly weed in the States,
is a perennial little known in this country. It has warm orange flowers.
In front is a flowering grass, *Achnatherum calamagrostis*.

What an extraordinary member of an extraordinary genus is *Senecio pulcher*. Whatever will it think of next? Brilliant magenta daisy rays surrounding a loud, declamatory yellow disc. Nothing could be more vulgar. I dote on it. It is an evergreen perennial, a foot or so tall, and astonishingly hardy but not quick to increase. Would you have guessed that it hailed from Uruguay? Perhaps, after seeing *S. smithii*, you should, but I did not.

To take the taste away, here's a harmony. *Asclepias tuberosa* is just about the same shade of orange as *Crocosmia* 'Solfatare', and both are 15 or 18 inches tall, but then come the differences. The asclepias has open corymbs of flowers with intriguing horned processes in the centre. The crocosmia is an old-fashioned (and rather weakly) montbretia, its flowers in spikes set among bronze-tinted spear leaves.

These have to stop flowering by the end of the month in order to make way for an entirely different colour palette. The bright, even loud pink of the bulb *Nerine × bowdenii* has ever struck me as untypical of autumn. What to set it with, or against? I find that *Aster amellus* 'Violet Queen', which is an unusually bright shade of purple in a michaelmas daisy, makes a good

In colours far from what we consider autumnal, these two are well matched:
the amaryllis-related bulb, *Nerine × howdenii*, and an *Aster amellus* michaelmas daisy
requiring no support, 'Violet Queen'.

Left: Cutting back the old foliage of *Liriope muscari* in spring
makes it look far smarter when flowering. *Colchicum* 'The Giant' has a much
shorter flowering season, but I like them in tandem while it lasts.

Right: My *Crocus nudiflorus* grow in the Upper Moat, and are gradually spreading.
Their strong colouring looks good against grass, but we give the latter its second cut
shortly before the crocuses flower, so that they do not appear half smothered.

companion. And I have lately added (though its season is shorter than the others) the magenta *Aster novae-angliae* 'Alma Potschke'.

Quite a number of bulbs flower in the autumn and the season makes their springlike freshness especially welcome. There is, for instance, the flower of the west wind, *Zephyranthes candida*, which is another Uruguayan. White crocus flowers above dark green rush leaves. I sometimes offset it with a small-flowered narrow-leaved bedding calceolaria, a form of *Calceolaria integrifolia*. It is a sharp, clear yellow.

I have colchicums in several parts of the garden. In the High Garden, 'The Giant' (typical rose-mauve) is grouped in front of the blue-mauve spikes of *Liriope muscari*. But the latter bleaches in the sun. I need to get this couple somewhere shadier. Colchicums are not fussy. The most striking of them all is *Colchicum speciosum* 'Album', with white goblets of considerable substance. It looks well with the grey filigree of *Artemisia canescens*, but the latter is apt to grow straggly in the early part of the season when the colchicum's foliage is voluminous. It might be sensible to wait until this had been removed and then to plant a grey bedder like *Helichrysum petiolatum* to do a filling-in job for the rest of the season.

The two autumn crocuses that grow best for me are *Crocus speciosus* and *C. nudiflorus*, though neither of them self-sows. I have to do most of the work in spreading them around and I have achieved a lot. *C. nudiflorus* has sturdy purple flowers and a stoloniferous habit. Its area of concentration is in the Upper Moat, and we give the grass here its second cut in mid-September so that the crocus does not appear to be swamped when it shows through. *C. speciosus*, with its dark veining, gives a blue impression and has prominent scarlet stigmas. Its 'stems' (perianth tubes, really) are long and frail so that the flower is often seen reclining, but this doesn't worry me. Biggest concentrations are in the meadow areas in front of the house, but some ten years ago (in 1976) I had a big planting out session by the Horse Pond, so I hope they'll make a spectacle there some day.

I don't think I shall ever make much of a splash with *Leucojum autumnale*, which grows in the Barn Garden, but it is a pet in its modest way with its little pink-flushed white bells, and it is an easy bulb to grow. Hardly ground cover though. You need to weed meticulously by hand in its environs.

Cyclamen have the quality of bulbs, and like many such, *Cyclamen hederifolium* starts its growing season by flowering, in mauvy pink or white. In my mother's day it was known as *C. neapolitanum* and she liked to call it sow bread (to annoy me), this being one of its vernacular names. I have never tried its tubers out as fodder for any kind of pig, and I'm sure she never did even when our sty was occupied. She was immensely fond of raising cyclamen from seed and planting out the resulting seedlings in all kinds of likely and unlikely places (as she did snowdrops), where most of them remain, for, once established, they are incredibly long lived. One of hers, a white, she wedged between two rocks at the base of a low wall on the lower terrace (a nice spot to sit when you're half-way round the garden), and its tuber, when unadorned by leaves, looks exactly like a squat toad. Most of her cyclamen are under the bay tree by the front path. She removed its lowest branches to make a bed for them.

I should like to be able to grow the Scarborough lily, *Vallota speciosa*, as a hardy bulb, and William Robinson says that it can be done. But although the bulbs survive well enough in a suitably warm spot outside, they do not produce their flowers in time to beat the winter. But I have them in pots (my whole stock was once wiped out by narcissus fly in the greenhouse), and when they start flowering I either bring them indoors or else stand them outside the porch. But the main September display here (unless I have been nodding, because stock continually needs to be renewed from seed if one is to keep ahead of virus disease) is by *Lilium formosanum*, which I plant three to a 7- or 8-inch pot. Its slender white trumpets and grassy foliage are the height of refinement, and they smell delicious at night *(p. 142)*.

Although I constantly ring the changes with my annuals, I have my favourites, and they are mostly of a kind that will keep the garden lively right through September and often through October also. On the heavyweight side there is *Nicotiana sylvestris*. As I raise it without heat and the seedlings are slow in the early stages, it does not really get into the swing of things until well into August. A proud-looking plant with handsome, rich green paddle leaves and pure white, long-tubed flowers that smell deliciously at night. It should grow 6 ft tall. I find this a useful replacement for foxgloves, and it favours moist shade. *Cosmos bipinnatus* will grow to 5 ft and makes suitable replacements for foxgloves or lupins. Especially good is the white 'Purity', with pale green filigree foliage. The imposing, zinnia-like *Tithonia rotundifolia* is the richest shade of orange and is shaped like a Mexican hat, but it needs a good summer to do itself justice. Big plants are also made by African marigolds, mallows and spider flowers, *Cleome spinosa*.

At the 2 ft level there is the undwarfed *Ageratum houstonianum*, whose mauve contrasts well with the yellow or orange of marigolds. Or, indeed, with the pale acid yellow pouches of *Calceolaria mexicana*, which seeds itself from year to year. I wonder if these three hobnob with one another in the wild? They're all Mexicans. So is *Cuphea miniata* 'Firefly', which makes a

There is beautiful detail in the flowers of *Linum grandiflorum* 'Rubrum',
an annual flax mixed in with other ingredients in the Long Border.

bushy, foot-tall plant that opens its cherry red, wavy-petalled flowers over a
long season.

I find it hard to resist a sowing of *Anagallis linifolia* in the deep blue
selection. It is a large-flowered pimpernel that opens to the sun; so rich and
intense a colour that it is often mistaken for a gentian. That would go well
with the 12–15 inch *Linum grandiflorum* 'Rubrum' somewhere behind it.
Again its warm red flowers open to the sun and they are beautifully marked.
The plant looks rather spindly early in the season, but steadily branches and
broadens.

Of many of these, and of a number of perennials also, I save my own seeds
– of the nicotiana, malope, white cosmos, cuphea and linum, for instance.
The pimpernel does not ripen good seed in our climate. I spend several
sessions on collecting seed heads as they ripen from the *Alstroemeria ligtu*
hybrids, putting them in a shoe box in a sunny window with a sheet of

newspaper over them to restrain the exploding capsules. *Salvia patens* 'Cambridge Blue' is a favourite bedding plant, and although I save its tubers I also like to grow seedlings as a second string. The seeds ripen over a long period and are not nearly as prolific as in the straight dark blue species.

Perhaps my most important seed collecting is of *Geranium wallichianum* 'Buxton's Blue'. We never have enough plants of this lovely perennial to sell, and nowhere can you buy the seed in any quantity. That is the only feasible method of propagation. The plants have to be returned to again and again. I like to clean the seed as I collect it, which saves trouble later on but means that I'm on my knees for long spells in front of those plants. They are at their most beautiful now, having started to flower in July. Blue saucers with white centres and purple anthers. The leaves, marbled in shades of green, are also a great asset. Collecting their seed continues into November.

Many of the shrubs that run to seed are colourful with berries. In most cases the birds see to it that they do not long remain so. Earliest of the whitebeams to ripen is *Sorbus* × *hostii*, truly described by Bean as lustrous red in fruit. But the display lasts a mere two or three days before a blackbird strips it. Perhaps I enjoy it all the more for knowing that it won't last.

Rosa moyesii and *R. setipoda* on the Long Border fare a good deal better. *R. rugosa* 'Alba', with large globular hips held conveniently below eye level (in the Orchard Garden), is spectacular and only destroyed when greenfinches decide to make a meal of the seeds. But they're pretty perfunctory about this. Funnily enough the Japanese wineberries, *Rubus pheonicolasius*, with their pretty clusters of sticky, raspberry-like fruits, ripen these to dark crimson and are often ignored by birds. I would agree that they have little flavour.

I make sure that the autumn-fruiting raspberries are safe in a cage (and not more than one blackbird shut in with them!), and the cage is locked, but not against birds. By far the most prolific of these raspberries is the yellow 'Fallgold'. Bright red though small-fruited 'Heritage' is the prettiest, while 'Zeva' has the best flavour.

I raise quite a number of outdoor tomatoes without having any pride in my prowess as a grower. I'm always late off the mark in planting them out and then I forget to pinch and train them when I should. There will be some, for salads, by now, and undoubtedly 'Gardener's Delight' has the best flavour. I only wish it was a bigger fruit. My principal tomato ambition is to have enough to be able to make a batch or two of the really excellent ripe tomato chutney that was my mother's speciality. So good to eat with cold meat throughout the year. To this end a large-fruited tomato that's easily blanched is essential, and I grow a 'Marmande' or beefsteak type. They ripen enough in every other year, on average. Thin-skinned, yellow 'Golden Sunrise' tomatoes are good in their way and of moderate size, but they are very wet. A fleshy fruit is more satisfactory. In any case, the colouring of a typical orange-red tomato is unbeatable. For culinary purposes a yellow tomato is far too anaemic. Here is the chutney recipe:

4 lb apples	$\frac{1}{2}$ oz powdered ginger
6 lb ripe tomatoes	1 teaspoon cayenne pepper
4 lb brown sugar	(I use even less)
1 lb sultanas	4 oz finely chopped onions or shallots
2 oz salt	2 pints malt vinegar

Peel, core and slice the apples, and *then* weigh them. Cook these first, separately. Skin the tomatoes by dipping them in hot water, and chop them roughly. Put all the ingredients in a preserving pan and boil for 1 hour or more until the mixture thickens. Store in broad-mouthed jars in a cool place.

Gourds and cucumbers are at their most luxuriant and prolific. By growing the gourds on a different site each year their tendency to mildew is minimized. I particularly like the vivid colouring and amazing shape of the Turbans, but also grow a mixture that includes the warted kinds. In fact it's a good plan to save seed from your favourites. They last the winter through in bowls and dishes in the house *(p. 182)*.

The cucumbers are grown on last year's compost heap, made from all the meadow grass collected. We quite often get mushrooms in this, too. Perhaps I ought to make sure of them by sowing some spawn, but there's always a crop of wild ones in a small field (it used to be our vegetable garden when we were a big family) not twenty yards distant, whenever the weather is right. Drought followed by warm rains gives the best results.

Even better than mushrooming, I enjoy blackberrying, and the last ten days of September is usually the right time to collect berries that are sufficiently pectin-rich to set bramble jelly without too much anxiety. Later pickings will be OK for deep-freezing for pies and crumbles.

Of course, prolific bramble hedges and good farming don't go hand in hand. A good stretch should enable me to pick at least four pounds, even five, in an hour. I only need Tulip and my thoughts for company. It is a most satisfying occupation.

October

---◆---

REA D I N G what has gone before, I wonder whether I have not made it
seem as though I live with my dog in a kind of cell, wherein I lead a
detached existence largely divorced from the interruptions of the outer
world. This is far from being the case, and if it is the impression given this
must be because writing is, of necessity, a solitary occupation. The sufficiently uninterrupted time to write a book can only be found in January and
February, and while it lasts I revel in the recollection of such moments of
solitude and reverie as can be snatched at other times of the year. They are
precious, but it is quite difficult to find the time, for instance, for those few
hours of blackberrying.

When your home is your workshop you are always exposed, whatever
you may be doing, to interruption. And much of this is welcome. Of the
20,000 visitors who annually come through our gate, some will become my
friends. They are kindred spirits and they make the effort of keeping a place
like Dixter going seem worth while. And I have a huge correspondence
linked to this. I write to those with whom I want to substantiate a first
acquaintance, and to those whom I shall eventually meet through having first
corresponded. I have a lot of house guests, too, and I enjoy cooking, which
helps that side to being social. I love sharing Dixter and it's a pleasure to think
that people like coming. I find travel stimulating too, especially when it is in
connection with my horticultural profession. That's another way to make
friends of others on my wavelength, though I never want travel to take me
away from my base, my *raison d'être*, too much.

Anyway, from April to September the moments when there is time to
pause and take stock are few. In October there is a change. It is an extremely
busy work month. We are sending parcels to mail-order customers again,
and we are, as we were last month, propagating like fury.

I leave the propagation of all those tender perennials that are safest
overwintered under frost-free glass until quite late. My greenhouse is not

Opposite: *Aronia arbutifolia* 'Erecta' colours briefly and vividly in late October,
but is usually quietly pleasing and takes up little lateral space.

very large and I want these cuttings to be as thick in it as possible; just rooted, but merely ticking over and not in a state to require more soil or more air space until March or April.

Such, then, as fuchsias, gazanias, *Convolvulus mauritanicus*, the tender helichrysums, *Felicia amelloides*, *Aster pappei*, bedding verbenas and penstemons, *Lavatera olbia*, osteospermums, greys like *Senecio leucostachys*, *S. cineraria*, *Centaurea gymnocarpa*, and many more are struck in a cold but double-walled, double-glazed frame and transferred from that in November or December to the greenhouse for the winter. Meanwhile the greenhouse has been completely emptied and washed in readiness.

The shrubs that we propagated last month, and some of them this, are hydrangeas, cistus, ceanothus, *Osmanthus delavayi*, *Genista lydia*, hebes (quite late), helianthemums, thyme, savory, lavender, rosemary. Some of these, like the evergreen ceanothus, are the safer for being overwintered in the greenhouse. All, wherever they are, receive a protective fungicide spraying once a week, using a rotation of three active ingredients, Benomyl, Captan and Rovral, so as to prevent fungal diseases, especially botrytis, from taking hold at the rather low temperatures at which we operate.

In the garden we at last have time to start clipping the yew hedges. I would prefer to have this under way from August, but we're too busy then with grass cutting and with keeping on top of weeds.

Although I don't overhaul my borders until the spring, there are many special upheavals and renewals that it is good to get done in October if the weather is kind, and there is spring bedding to start moving in, and bulbs to be planted, if not all of them this month then by early next. But we close the house and gardens to the public half-way through October, and that gives us more time to consider our own affairs and to plan ahead.

Compared to what has gone before, the mood of October seems wonderfully relaxed. 'What is October like in China?' I asked a lady who had just been there in that month. 'October is beautiful everywhere,' she replied. World-wide around the temperate northern hemisphere, that is true. Years ago I read an article in a gardening magazine about Finland in October; an improbable subject, yet so evocative that I wrote to the author to say how I had enjoyed it. She turned out to be half Finn and to have lived her childhood there. We've been firm friends these twenty years, now.

It is as foolish to have a favourite month or season as it is to have a favourite flower. The flower of this moment, or this moment now and for itself, are

Opposite: The Horse Pond in autumn takes on an air of reflective tranquillity.

our favourites while they last. Then we move on. So, foolishly, October has always been my favourite month. It appeals to my imagination. Boisterous winds no longer matter. Falling leaves chase around in a joyous dance and I never get over the childhood delight of scuffling my feet through drifts of them.

But there is also a great calm about October. The turmoils of the growing season are past. The light is soft, glowing and kind, the days not yet uncomfortably short or cold. The plants have made their preparations for a necessary rest. Even the growth of weeds slows down, and a sense of unhurrying peace descends. No longer that insistent now or never feeling. If a job isn't done today or this week it will, in many (not all) cases, wait. The year's planting season for trees and shrubs stretches ahead and can be reckoned in months.

Most autumn colour reaches its climax in the second half of the month. It is then that we visit such famous spots as Westonbirt arboretum and Sheffield Park Gardens. Intensity of colour varies a great deal from year to year, but most of the great excitements are provided by exotica from China, Japan and North America. Our own contribution is mousier but has its own charm. I keep telling myself, and my friends from the north keep telling me, that I must visit Scotland in October, when birches and aspens turn to pale gold and the deer grass and bracken to russet shades.

I have aspens (three!) and birches myself, on the bank overlooking the Horse Pond. The aspens make a delightful fluttering sound which you notice when reclining with your eyes closed nearby, but it is too cold for basking here any more; the sun barely strikes these north-facing banks. I have to seek a south-facing slope in the orchard.

We have no consciously planned autumn tints at Dixter; just touches here and there that rather take one by surprise. In all but gardens of park-like extent, I think it is a mistake to plan for autumn colour unless the plants that are to provide it also make some positive contribution earlier on. Autumn colour in any one plant is extremely short-lived, even supposing it develops at all. Our clay soil doesn't favour it, but there are small pleasures such as, for instance, when some of the cranesbills flare up; certain euphorbias too, while the little bush cherry, *Prunus glandulosa* 'Alba Plena' *(p. 68)* never fails to change to peachy pink. Four or five days and it is over.

I would not be without the rowan, *Sorbus* 'Joseph Rock', which I can see from my bathroom window as it changes to deep flame red. It also, in some years, bears crops of deep yellow berries, but they are among the blackbird's favourites. One bird can easily and quickly demolish the entire crop.

The hawthorn, *Crataegus* × *prunifolia*, is an excellent small tree.
Its foliage colours before falling, then the birds eat the haws from
the crown downwards – a blackbird can be seen at work here; Tulipa below.
A frosty morning – I've cheated. This was taken late in November.

Less quickly our *Crataegus* × *prunifolia*, of which I have two mature trees. If their flower buds were left untouched by bullfinches in the spring, they crop heavily with masses of deep red haws which load their branches to the ground. Their foliage can colour well too, but rather patchily. The mistle thrushes sometimes take a fancy to this crop, and the starlings, but mostly blackbirds. They start stripping from the crown of the tree and work downwards. Those fruits that are blown to the ground they never touch. Their mothers never taught them that it's wicked to be wasteful.

We do not for long enjoy the *Cotoneaster horizontalis* berries that are ripe now, but the gobbling birds are an entertainment in themselves.

It's funny how there are some berries that the birds never touch, not in my garden, anyway. They must in nature, if berry production means anything. I don't think berry colour is relevant; or if it is to one bird, it has a different relevance to another. What could look more appetizing than the clusters of shining red berries on *Viburnum opulus* 'Compactum', the guelder rose in my Long Border? But they ripen in late August and hang till they drop in December.

My female *Schizandra rubriflora (p. 88)* has 9-inch-long dangles of red berries in September and October, but it's the wind that eventually blows them off and the seedlings germinate immediately underneath. I never see a bird in my *Celastrus*, which has bright orange seeds that are revealed when the yellow capsule splits open, right at the end of the month and as the last of its yellow leaves are falling.

You can see now why the dogwood, *Cornus alba*, is so named. Its berries are white and I know the birds spread them around, as seedlings will appear anywhere in the garden. These dogwoods, by the Horse Pond's margin, flare up briefly before shedding their coarse leaves to reveal naked carmine stems. They reflect cheeringly in the water's surface when it is not too ruffled, or frozen.

The water is very clear now, and you can see the green underwater cloud forms of *Hottonia palustris*, the water violet. Emerging 3 ft out of the water, the radiating papyrus spokes of *Cyperus longus* are still green and glossy.

The smell of autumn is typically sharp. I don't know what causes it but I always imagine fungi to have greatest responsibility. If the soil is damp there'll be crops of toadstools under the birches; *Boletus*, *Amanita rubescens* – the blusher, whose flavour I'm none too keen on – and the wicked-looking red-and-white fly agaric, *Amanita muscaria*.

There are many good incidents and, indeed, features in my October garden, and if the weather is right, and also the kind of person looking at it, I feel no need to apologize. But there's one set piece, reaching its peak mid-month, of which I feel really proud. In what used to be the Lavender Garden, where there are as many as eighteen topiary peacocks, I have double hedges, linking them, of *Aster lateriflorus* 'Horizontalis'. The lavender didn't really like our heavy soil and was always dying out in patches, so ten years ago I replaced it with this michaelmas daisy, which has always been in the garden and has a widely branching, almost shrub-like habit but grows no more than 3 ft tall. Its daisies are tiny, with backwards-pointing, off-white rays and prominent purple discs. The foliage itself is purplish. Flowering starts in early September, and slowly gathers momentum until by mid-October there

Left: The twining climber, *Celastrus orbiculatus*, is noted for its orange and yellow
fruits *(p. 23)*, but its foliage turns clear yellow before falling.

Right: The bushy michaelmas daisy, *Aster lateriflorus* 'Horizontalis',
which reaches its peak in October but looks good for most of the year.

is a seething mass of many thousand daisies. In front of them, and linking
them with the paths, I have strips of the mat-forming *Polygonum vaccini-*
folium, which carries cohorts of little rosy mauve pokers at about 3 or 4 inches
in the autumn. The two plants' flowerings absolutely coincide. The display
fades slowly but retains its bones right through the winter. When touched by
hoar frost, the asters flower again.

Another aster that I'm fond of is *A. ericoides* 'Esther', which I have at the
front of the Long Border. It is only 2 ft tall, with a graceful, spraying habit
and bright green foliage all through the summer. Its flowers are pinky
mauve. I must also put in a good word for a naturalized michaelmas daisy of
the small-flowered *ericoides* type which grows along the fence between the
Horse Pond and the entrance drive. That is 4 ft tall but never flops.

That I so often take photographs in the garden in fine October weather is no act of bravado. Consider, for instance, the corner at the bottom of the Long Border where I was saying that it is pleasant to sit on the raised terrace wall. There is the open-sided loggia on its tile pillars to your left and the solar wing of the house in front. This piece of garden used to be enclosed by a castellated box hedge. The enclosure was, for a few years (but not from the start), a knot garden, but we never really liked it. Eventually I had the hedge out, and the whole area can now be seen as one unit. I try to keep to shrubs of no more than 4 or 5 ft high within it, except for a fastigiate *Aronia arbutifolia* 'Erecta', which grows to 7 ft and is flaming now. Autumn is its big moment, but it is always quietly pleasing.

A major feature of recent years has been a bush ivy propagated from the adult wood of *Hedera canariensis* 'Variegata'. It grew amazingly fast; in a matter of seven years, to 6 ft high and a good deal more across. It was particularly beautiful in October and November when covered with umbels of blossom buds. If they were later frosted, it didn't really matter, but in some years they would open and flower before the frosts arrived. This bush was severely maimed in the 1985 winter and I had to cut it back. It broke, low down, but all its shoots were of the juvenile, climbing (or trailing) kind. It wasn't ground cover that I was seeking but a bushy corner feature, so the shrub had to be extracted. I have a young one of my own propagation, from adult wood, to take its place.

Behind it is a large self-sown *Skimmia japonica* – a female, and there is a male at hand to pollinate it. The skimmia's new crop of large red berries has just now ripened. There is a grove of hydrangeas, past their best but still beautiful as they fade. Then a patch of the fuchsia 'Mme Cornelissen', with rather elegant leaves and a huge crop of red and white flowers. Earlier it does practically nothing (inhibited, no doubt, by capsid bugs feeding on the young shoots), but at this late moment suddenly comes into its own.

Against the terrace wall there is the inestimable *Daphniphyllum macropodum*, which I described in January. Against the projecting piece of house which is a staircase, *Hydrangea petiolaris* changes to bright yellow before shedding. It catches the late afternoon sun.

Whereas some October flowers are largely an aftermath of summer, there are others which belong entirely to this season. Pampas grass is one of the latter. I have two large clumps in the Barn Garden. They are well separated, but the eye can take them in simultaneously. When you have only one clump of a thoroughly self-centred plant like this, as I originally did, it looks odd, as though it had strayed from outer space. A second clump makes all the

I have two clumps of the pampas, *Cortaderia selloana* 'Pumila', in the Barn Garden.
This dwarfish clone has upright brushes to 6 ft.

difference. Even so, within the context of a relatively small, enclosed
compartment, really tall pampas plants would have been overpowering, so I
have the fairly dwarf *Cortaderia selloana* 'Pumila' (from Margery Fish). It
grows some 6 ft tall and bears a great number of upright brushes, but there is
some variation in the height to which they grow and that is welcome.

I have it in mind to bring *Kniphofia rooperi* into this picture when I can work
up enough stock (the '85 winter didn't help). Given me by Patrick Synge, this
is an October-flowering poker with rather dense, squat spikes, orange in

bud, opening yellow. I would like to have the torch lily not only next to one of the pampas clumps but also forming the foreground from a viewpoint on the other side of the Barn Garden, so that you are looking over a squad of 3-ft spikes to those that stand in the distance. The drawback to this plan is that the kniphofia's season is quite short, and it is the kind of ugly plant that you don't want to be much aware of for the rest of the year.

A number of late-flowering grasses are now in bloom, especially if the summer was hot. It doesn't matter too much whether *Miscanthus sinensis* 'Gracillimus', *M.s.* 'Strictus' (a zebra grass) and *M.s.* 'Variegatus' flower or not, because their foliage is good, but it's nice when they do. *M.s.* 'Silver Feather' can be relied upon, and has been flowering in its Long Border position near the yew archway since early last month. It deserves prominence, but since it has rather a length of leg (7 ft) I have planted a *Pinus mugo* in front of it. I learned how well dwarf conifers and flowering grasses look together when in the East Coast United States, but this idea came to me before my visit!

Hakonechloa macra 'Aureola' and *Molinia caerulea* 'Variegata' are other grasses grown for their foliage but with a welcome flowering now, and I have lately added, on a prominent corner in the Orchard Garden, *M.c.* 'Altissima Windspiel', the slender height of whose flowering stems is its principal asset. Meanwhile the dying inflorescences of *Calamagrostis acutiflora* 'Stricta' are as beautiful as ever, though changing slowly all the while.

A froth of spiky white blossom above scalloped leaves characterizes the flowering of *Saxifraga fortunei* in October, but you never see enough of it. I must remedy that, some day. It might work in with a drift of *Crocus speciosus*. Where I have the latter and *Nerine bowdenii* under the bay tree, they flower later than any other colony because it is so dry here. It is useful to know that you can make use of a dry patch in order to prolong a bulbous flower's season. It works for cyclamen also.

Tropaeolum tuberosum, with garlands and festoons of long-spurred, ochre-yellow flowers and orange veining in the centre, is naturally a late – all too late – autumn flowerer and I have the 'Ken Aslet' clone which starts in July and then flowers on. I find, however, that it flowers fairly reluctantly early on and is much freer in October. I don't trust its tubers in the garden through the winter, even near a wall, because they are vulnerably near the surface. Nasturtiums, *T. majus*, have a gorgeous and prolific last fling now, displaying themselves over the faded remnants of other plants in the Long Border. There is no more rewarding tropaeolum than this.

Though not as hardy as other periwinkles, you are unlikely ever to lose *Vinca difformis*, and its natural exuberance will soon restore its fortunes after a

The climbing, tuberous-rooted *Tropaeolum tuberosum* flowers rather later than one would like. This earlier-starting clone, 'Ken Aslet', is still at its best quite late.

bad winter. It is a lovely plant and at its best in October with a huge display of palest, ice blue blossom. The end of each petal looks as though it has been cut diagonally with scissors. It will continue to flower in mild spells throughout the winter, but looks pinched and pallid after frost. Sometimes it gathers its forces for a final flowering in late spring, even in June, but it never stood a chance of an award in the R.H.S. *Vinca* trial, because March and April, when the trial was inspected, are not its season of beauty. If it is awards you are after it doesn't pay to be nonconformist, but gardeners can love *V. difformis* the more for bringing its springlike freshness into autumn.

No one could call *Buddleia auriculata* springlike, but fresh in its October season, most certainly. It is evergreen, and unusual in a buddleia for its slender glossy leaves not including a trace of coarseness. It needs a warm wall position and may attain a considerable height here. Its panicles of tiny buff flowers are deliciously scented on the air. The plant suckers and will regenerate from roots, so that once properly established you are unlikely to lose it. Mine has survived many vicissitudes.

So has *Eryngium pandanifolium* (*E. decaisneanum*), which I have never quite lost though there have been nasty moments. I have it in the Long Border where it soars to 8 ft in October with branching candelabra of minute, dove mauve flowers above long, saw-edged evergreen foliage. It is a magnificent

'Lionel Fortescue' is the first of the *Mahonia* × *media* hybrids to flower. Bees flock to it. Its habit is upright and leggy, so it should be pruned back firmly each April.

species and truly architectural, but not for those who hanker after eyefuls of colour. This eryngium's best protection is its own foliage. Established colonies keep the soil very dry beneath them, which is a sovereign recipe for winter hardiness.

The first of the winter series of mahonias is out: *Mahonia* × *media* 'Lionel Fortescue'. The shrub has an upswept habit, which should be checked by quite heavy pruning every spring, and its yellow blossom racemes point upwards strongly. They continue opening throughout November, and on any still, sunny day you'll find them covered with honey bees.

It's difficult to know just when to write of bamboos, whose season of looking positively good is so long, but most of them are at their smartest now, especially *Phyllostachys*, of which I keep collecting more kinds. They deserve a position of prominence, and a dark background helps enormously if it can be found, but that is not always possible. However, I'm greatly pleased with my placing of *P. nigra* (the black-stemmed type plant), given me by Archie Skinner from Sheffield Park Gardens. As you walk through the Orchard Garden from the Long Border and are beginning to mount the steps to the High Garden, there's a splendidly architectural view to your left, with the big, clipped topiary yew (once a tree), a yew archway and hedges curving to right and left; the house and oast buildings behind. I have sited the bamboo to left front of the yews. It hasn't been there many years, but is happy and beginning to make its mark. The Chilean *Chusquea culeou* makes an imposing brush of foliage in front of the house.

The placing of an important plant is not easy. Being a compulsive plantsman, it's usual for me to acquire the plant first and look for the right position afterwards. I like to go round the garden with a sympathetic friend, with the question constantly at the front of our minds: where shall it go? Sometimes the friend gets the answer first, more often I do, as I should, being on the spot all the time. The main thing is to have been forced to concentrate on the one problem till it has been solved. I find that less easy by myself, when I'm all too easily distracted. It could work the other way round but it doesn't.

The only apple that I'm concerned to take a crop from nowadays is 'Bramley's Seedling', of which some enormous standards, planted in the early 1920s, are located near our top boundary beyond the High Garden (off the plan). I say enormous, but in fact it is only the trees nearest the fruit cage and vegetable garden which are really large as they have a greater depth of soil. This deteriorates in the hinterland where honey fungus is also rife, so a few more gaps develop every year. We leave the apple picking as late as we dare because they put on a lot of weight at the last, but there's always a risk of a gale spoiling our plans. The best fruit is at the top of the trees, where we can't reach it even from ladders. Anyone in their senses would cut their tops off the trees but that would spoil their appearance which, at blossom time, counts a lot with me. The result is that I eat windfalls right up till Christmas. The big chaps have to fall sooner or later, and even with a bruise on one side they are profitable to deal with in the kitchen. I like stewed apples for breakfast every morning and so, I notice, do most of my friends. A few, evidently put off the fruit in early youth, are sniffy.

There's a tremendous range of vegetables to choose from this month, when the summer varieties, like beans, overlap with the first of winter's, like celeriac. If the lettuces falter, as they are sure to sooner or later, I hope to replace them with sugarloaf chicory, a marvellous chewy salading that needs no blanching but hearts up well if we've grown it properly. Always a big IF, I'm afraid.

With farewell to October it's farewell to the swallows, and I regret their departure more than any bird's, though a few will hang on till the end of the month. I'm always squinting at the sky, hoping to light upon a couple as they hawk for insects.

November

W HAT a strange mix-up is November. The weather doesn't know its mind, and one year's will differ wildly from another's. On average it is our wettest month, with 3.85 inches (we've been keeping rainfall records since 1913), but what averages usually mean is that there were 7 inches or there were less than 2.

In the old days, before the drainage schemes that have quite lately been installed, we could look down from our hilltop heights (only 180 ft, actually) on a huge lake which covered the whole Rother valley marsh – approximately a mile wide at this point. It was worth seeing from our roof, which also gives a view of warm red tiles, wet and gleaming, and patches of red berries and carmine foliage from *Cotoneaster horizontalis* in the garden below *(p. 176)*. It was all marvellously scenic on a blue day following rain, and exciting on the marsh itself, with many migrant waterfowl moving in to take advantage of the muddy waters.

But in the dry years there'll be a lot of fine weather and great garden activity of a creative sort right through to the month's end.

The trouble with November is that the days are now so short that it really hurts, no matter how we manipulate the clock. Just when you've got well stuck into a job, night closes in. 'Tomorrow,' you think and plan, but when tomorrow comes there's been a frost, so that you cannot get on with planting till it's out of the ground; or else a fine drizzle coats everything with slime – tools, hands, clothes as well as plants (never try to plant wallflowers when their leaves are wet) – and efficiency and tolerance are drastically reduced.

We'll have our first frost of the autumn, and if this is sharp it is quite dramatic. Following a still clear night, all the leaves from our mulberry and the ash trees will drop within a couple of hours to form a dense carpet beneath.

Our propagating frames are under ash trees in the frameyard. They are still full of cuttings. In the summer we are glad of the broken shade – never too

Opposite: In the Barn Garden, wet roofs gleaming.
Yucca and phormium in the foreground, *Miscanthus sinensis* 'Variegatus' in the distance.

171

heavy – which a canopy of ash leaves provides as soon as the sun has risen high enough to get them between it and the frame lights. But now that the sun is weak we want our cuttings to receive every scrap of light that's going, so the ash leaves' falling is a great release. They don't fall all together in most years, and I rather like the companionable tapping that their stalks make on the potting shed roof while I'm busy with something at the bench.

The oaks hold their leaves till the very end of the month, but ripe acorns are falling. This is especially noticeable where the trees overhang the dark Lower Moat, and acorns plop as they fall in.

My hydrangeas present a hideous sight once frosted, because their leaves are blackened on the bushes and hang like dismal scarecrow drapery for weeks afterwards.

Yet there are qualities special to November. The medlar outside the back gate is a fine sight, its leaves colouring so warmly that I always want to rush out with my camera to record this brief and magic moment. In most years it is loaded with its quaint brown fruit, each with a large creased eye surrounded by the whiskers that were the flower's calyx. Beautiful things and pleasant to handle. It seems sad they should be so useless. Barely edible raw even when soft and bletted. I tried making medlar jelly once, but it was a disaster from which I have yet to recover.

We shouldn't really grumble at a fruit for being useless. If it is a pleasure to look at and touch it has already served us well. Another such is the wild pear in front of the house, whose flowering I recorded in May. It is now smothered in small, almost globular fruits that have only a hint of a neck to show they are pears rather than the crabs for which they are usually mistaken. Eventually they become quite sweet but wholly insipid. Whenever there's a gale the lawn is strewn with them, and whoever is mowing has a lot of preliminary shovelling on hand. But in some years, autumn gales fail to materialize. The pear's leaves drop around 10 November, and a magical crop of luminous yellow fruits, hanging in heavy swags, is fully revealed. When these fall, mowing is no longer important. Neither is tidiness. I leave them to our blackbirds *(p. 176)*.

One would not say that this was a much treed garden, yet leaves are the undertow to our November lives. On the lawns they don't worry me much unless they're obviously taking light from the grass. Before we gather and spread them as a mulch around the rhododendrons, I like to wait until the wind has herded them into convenient drifts. But there's one leaf, the largest of them all, which we never have to bother about. Fig leaves in no time shrivel to nothing; there is no fibre in them. Did Adam realize that?

My medlar never fails to change to warm russet tones.

'A terrible year for leaves,' said a friend's old gardener when he couldn't think of any worse disaster to grumble about, and there always had to be something. I must say, the innocence of gardeners who think they'll save themselves trouble from fallen leaves by growing evergreens amazes me. An evergreen sheds as many leaves in a twelvemonth as a deciduous shrub or tree, but they are far more leathery and slower to rot down, and they generally fall in greatest profusion at a most inconvenient early summer season. At least their deciduous brethren have the decency to get it all done and over in a matter of six weeks.

I can't wait for the witch hazels and winter sweets to lose theirs, which are so notably clumsy, whereas the naked branches, once revealed, can be seen clustered with flower buds that will soon be cheering us enormously. Indeed, the first winter sweet (*Chimonanthus praecox*) blooms not unusually open

The grass, *Miscanthus sinensis* 'Silver Feather' (*left*), flowers in September
but retains its beauty for a long time.

before the end of the month. *Lonicera* × *purpusii*, with evergreenery in its
parentage, is slower to shed, but has it done before its main flowering season.

From now on I like to keep a large 'flower' arrangement going in the Great
Hall, because it lasts such a long time in the cool weather. *Fatsia japonica* and
Aucuba japonica 'Crotonifolia' will supply the necessary evergreen weight and
simplicity. Without this, deciduous branches readily turn fussy. I include half
a dozen pronged stems of dogwood and they provide anchorage for some of
the long trails of *Celastrus orbiculatus*, whose berries will last the winter
through. Spindle berries – orange and surrounded with a fleshy pink aril – are
a temptation, but they shrivel more quickly in water than outdoors. Privet
berries, from *Ligustrum* × *vicaryi*, last well, and their blackness sets off the
brighter colours. Perhaps a few grey heads from the pyramidal *Senecio
tanguticus* in seed, or from *Miscanthus sinensis* 'Silver Feather'.

My permanent big feature in the solar, upstairs, is the fern *Woodwardia radicans*. One plant will last me ten years in a 10-inch pot if I remember to water it (easy to forget in freezing winter's weather when the room is not in use) and feed it. The fronds are up to 5 ft long and spread outwards like wings, helped by a slender cane and stem tie to each of them. It stands in the north window and loves to be cool and sunless, so long as it receives plenty of light.

There's never any difficulty in picking a bunch of flowers in November. It is a meeting of the seasons, with many remnants from summer like *Achillea ×taygetea* and *Anthemis tinctoria*. Then there are the month's own goodies. I grow five kinds of Kaffir lilies, *Schizostylis coccinea*, and the last to open is the clear pink 'Viscountess Byng'. It goes well with *Serratula seoanei*, which is a kind of knapweed with a haze of small mauve thistle heads among purplish, deeply cut foliage. After flowering, the ripe seed heads open out into the likeness of a flower themselves, straw-coloured now and pretty right through to spring. The schizostylis has ixia-like flowers in 2-ft spikes. It's an easy genus to grow if your soil is stiff and on the heavy side.

More ingredients for our bunch could come from the winter jasmine, which starts to flower before it has shed its leaves, and this is also the irritating habit of *Viburnum × bodnantense* and *V. farreri*. Best to break their leaves off straight away. The most spring-like ingredient will be polyanthus, which always seem to be confused about the time of year.

There's a range of berries. The fruits on my magnolias arouse a good deal of curiosity from visitors long before they ripen. The grotesquely bulbous

Nice November teamwork when this form of the Kaffir lily, *Schizostylis coccinea* 'Viscountess Byng', combines with the mauve *Serratula seoanei*.

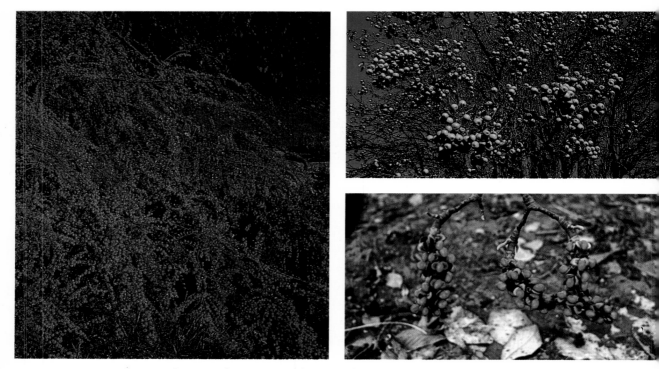

Winter fruits. *Left*: *Cotoneaster horizontalis* is spectacular in late November,
when the scarlet of its berries coincides with the carmine of its changing foliage.
Above right: The wild pear comes into its own again in autumn, especially if gales
hold off. *Below right*: The fruits of the magnolia are grotesquely appealing.

pods are often twisted and deformed, and they change from green to puce pink, then split to reveal scarlet-coated seeds. If you want to sow them for a bit of fun, remove the scarlet seed coat first (it inhibits quick germination) and leave the pots where frost can reach them. You should get some germination in the first spring.

Hollies will have developed their full berry colouring by the end of the month. We are surrounded by wild hollies. My principal tame tree within the garden – just about the best feature in the Long Border, taking the year round – is the slow-growing *Ilex × altaclarensis* 'Golden King', which has a yellow leaf margin and few prickles – a great consideration when weeding among fallen leaves. Despite its masculine name, this is a female, and a regular cropper at that. The berries are attractive at every stage of ripening. I remember an occasion when a potential customer saw the parent plant when its berries were still yellow. Thinking she would want them red, I assured her that they soon would be. However, it turned out that she wanted them to stay yellow, so I lost my customer. I was much younger then.

The obvious yellow-variegated evergreen with which to compare this holly, supposing you had to make a choice between the two, because both take up a good deal of space, is the considerably more popular *Elaeagnus pungens* 'Maculata'. The holly is slower-growing in youth, but, as is nearly always the way, the slow-growing shrub eventually makes the more beautiful specimen. The elaeagnus has, I admit (and I do grow it also), the brighter yellow variegation, and it can be a tremendously cheering sight on a sunny winter's day – almost like a patch of daffodils, in the distance. But it makes a large and clumsy bush. Its shoots have a way of branching at right angles or, indeed, at any angle so that they behave like ingrowing toenails. Pruning by thinning out helps, but can never be substitute for a natural shapeliness. Furthermore, it has a habit of reverting to plain green. Such branches need removing every year, otherwise they take over, being stronger growing than those with variegated leaves. It isn't a difficult job, if regularly performed, but the number of elaeagnus you see with large reverted patches bears witness that it is more often forgotten or ignored than not.

Some nurserymen are tempted to deal in grafted plants, because they make up so much more quickly in youth than those on their own roots. The plain-leaved understock is particularly given to suckering. Need I say more?

There is great satisfaction in seeing the garden take on the clean lines of winter, notwithstanding that I leave the overhauling of the borders until spring. The yew hedges and topiary look smart, especially on a frosty morning when their tops are white. John Ashbee starts the winter digging and achieves an amazing area in the one day a week he's with me. To my astonishment, he always digs uphill, starting a piece at its lowest point.

The areas of meadow are given their last cut, leaving the grass almost (not quite) as trim as the lawns. This will allow the small bulbs to show up to maximum advantage when they start flowering in the New Year. Also, tight cuts between July and November tend to discourage the coarser grasses and weeds in the turf. It is the finest grasses that profit.

This is the time when it is easiest to wield a bulb-planting tool, and I'll often establish a new colony of winter crocuses or (except that I now have enough) of *Camassia esculenta*. I should like to get the lanky *C. leichtlinii* into turf because when a bulb like this, which flops in a border, grows up among grass stems, they'll support and keep it upright.

I'll also move into a wild area some plant or other from my borders, where it self-sows or has taken up more space than it deserves. The globe flower,

Trollius, for instance, of which I have the pale yellow 'Canary Bird'. It flowers for too short a period to deserve much border space, but in the half-shaded leafy area where my rhododendrons are, that doesn't matter.

I also moved *Cardamine latifolia* from the borders, where it made too much leaf for the amount of rosy mauve lady's smock blossom that went with it. Now it grows like watercress in a piece of damp meadow, and even if it's as leafy as ever, the flowers are numerous enough to make a pretty display.

Columbines of the old-fashioned *Aquilegia vulgaris* type self-sow like crazy, but they can be moved into meadow, which is their natural habitat. I have failed to establish doronicums in the rather thin turf under trees where I feel they should succeed, but in some gardens, especially in the north, they are a *succès fou*. As you find yourself with surplus plant material, you'll be thinking, 'Where might I try this?' as well as, 'Who would like some of it?'

There's a lot of planting out of biennials (or of plants that I treat as biennials) to be done in the autumn. Myosotis are conspicuous by their absence. I content myself with those that self-sow among perennials in the borders. I may come back to them some day. There are some pleasing pink and, better still, white strains that it might be interesting to feature.

For the rest, here are the ones that frequently recur, though not in every year. Foxgloves (*Digitalis*), sown in April, pricked off in a box and lined out for the summer. *Verbascum olympicum* is given exactly the same treatment and makes enormous plants which eventually need staking individually. I have written of lupins, of which I use a mixed Russell strain. The seed germinates much earlier and more evenly for first being rubbed between sandpaper. *Hesperis matronalis*, sweet rocket; I find this shows up best, in a somewhat shady border, in a white strain, though this is imperfectly selected by the seedsmen. Honesty, *Lunaria annua*, is a close relation. Again I prefer the white, for bedding, and can collect my own self-sown seedlings to line out for the summer. Crucifers tend to have coarse roots and are not the easiest subjects for transplanting. Even wallflowers need care. It is worth compressing the soil to make a ball around the roots as you lift in order to transplant. Our heavy soil makes this easier than it would be on sand or chalk. Stocks, however, grow much more happily on the lighter soils, and I often have difficulty in overwintering the Bromptons. The secret, I think, is to spray them with a protective fungicide in late winter and again in early spring. If botrytis once sets in on a plant's foliage it rapidly spreads and kills.

Besides wallflowers, which are *Cheiranthus*, certain *Erysimum* lend themselves to bedding. The Siberian wallflower, for example, but I find the colouring of this just a bit too harsh and assertive in the mass. It is a beautiful,

Mixed borders retain a deal of interest well into winter, with specially strong
contributions from fading grasses and the distant hydrangea flower heads.

clean shade of orange, and the scent is delicious. We used to have plants that
self-sowed in paving cracks for many years. In this way you enjoy it without
having a bellyful. I must try and reorganize that. Then there is the low-
growing, mauve-flowered *E. linifolium*, still obtainable (though only just)
from Thomas Butcher of Shirley, Croydon. It makes a nice carpet to late-
flowering tulips. Sow, like wallflowers, in the open, but a month later, in
June, otherwise they'll flower at half cock in the autumn. It would be
interesting to know the parentage of the shrubby *Erysimum* 'Bowles's
Mauve'. It is sterile and must be propagated from cuttings. If these are struck
in May and subsequently lined out, they'll produce large plants for bedding
by the autumn and again look well with tulips or with a really late *Narcissus*
like the jonquil 'Tittle Tattle'.

I scarcely grow polyanthus any more. The shady bed where I most like to
have them is polyanthus sick. Half those bedded out in the autumn will be
dead by flowering time. I can't be bothered to change the soil. I sometimes do

auriculas, however, though they really require two seasons from a spring sowing to make a large plant.

Aquilegias are apt to be slow, but if you sow in March and bring the seedlings on without a check, eventually lining them out for the summer, they'll make up well for bedding in the autumn. Plants can be saved to do a second year (line them out after flowering, about the end of June), but should be discarded after that. Single colour strains are more effective than mixtures, but are not always easy to find, these days.

Of *Bellis*, the daisies, my favourites by far are the Pomponette strains (again in single colours: white, pink or red rather than mixtures) with quilled rays on small heads. The seed is small, so I sow in a box in July, prick off the seedlings, then line them out. By November they're splendid plants. Same treatment exactly for pansies or violas. I like yellow or blue viola strains (without faces) as a carpet to tulips.

Last but not least, the *Dianthus* tribe. Various seed strains of cottage pinks or of *D. alpinus* are to be had. If sown in April, pricked off and lined out for the summer (there'll be some flowering in the rows but not too much), they can be bedded in the autumn and will flower the following June and early July. I've never found the ideal bulb to go with these, although I've tried *Brodiaea laxa* and Dutch irises. Tulip foliage would be in a too obtrusively dying state to be suitable, by the time the pinks were flowering, but I always interplant sweet williams (*D. barbatus*) with tulips, so as to provide early interest. Sweet williams grow tall and entirely hide the dying tulips, which can be harvested when the sweet williams are thrown out at the end of July. Sow these in April and treat like the pinks.

Border carnations also. They'll make fat plants by the autumn and I love the glaucous colouring of their foliage. When bedded, I like to interplant them with *Tulipa eichleri*, which has glaucous leaves and brilliant red flowers, black at the base inside. There'll be no problem with dying tulip leaves, because carnations grow as tall as sweet williams. *But* – big snag, this – they are weak-stemmed and should really be given support with shortish pieces of brushwood just before they come into flower. They do make a lovely and unusual July feature and one, I think, worth working for, though not every year. I always reckon to replace them in late July with a late-sown annual.

I have a great weakness for *Dianthus* 'Rainbow Loveliness' (briefly mentioned in August), and am seldom without a patch of this. The flowers are deeply laced, the colours white, pinky mauve and deep carmine, the scent wonderfully sweet on the air. July is a good time to sow in a pot so as to have good plants by the autumn that yet don't weaken themselves by flowering

Mahonia × *undulata* changes to purple as the weather turns cold. Right, *Miscanthus sinensis* 'Strictus', and a dwarf bamboo, *Arundinaria viridistriata*, in front.

prematurely. Prick off, in a seed tray, then pot up individually in 3½-inch pots. From these you can choose whether to plant out in November or to delay till March. Flowering is in June. Some plants would survive to do a second year, but it's not worth offering them the chance. The brilliant red *Dianthus* 'Queen of Hearts' responds well to the same treatment.

Colder weather brings seasonal changes of colour in some evergreen foliage. My *Mahonia* × *undulata* turns from green to purple. That's never gloomy because it has such a light-reflecting gloss.

Conifers are apt to change more than most, although some of them, like *Juniperus sabina tamariscifolia* (two cascades of which I have in the Sunk Garden), not at all. *Chamaecyparis thyoides* 'Ericoides' turns from sea-green to purple, though it remains green where protected, within the bush. *Thuja occidentalis* 'Rheingold' turns a deep, old gold, especially on the sunny side of the bush. Sometimes you begin to wonder if it's dying, but it's not.

Whatever cold snaps there may be in November – and snow seems insultingly premature, but it does happen – I've never let it make me unduly gloomy. There's no need to feel, 'It may be like this for the next four months.' Big swings of temperature are the rule at this time of year but they presage nothing. Anything can happen next. I take it as it comes.

December

ALL the peoples of the temperate Northern Hemisphere celebrate the turning of the year, the passing of its shortest day, in December. Our excuses for celebration may be Christian or pagan, but whatever they are the break is welcome. Hope palpably lies ahead as the evenings begin to lengthen. True, we are only in the first month of winter and the worst of its discomforts and worries are yet to come, but winter has many saving graces and the gardener is well aware of them.

Not least of these is the very fact of not having to think too much about the garden, not in terms of the present, anyway. The seed catalogues nowadays flood in well before the holiday and provide happy hours of armchair browsing and speculation.

At last the weeds have almost ceased to grow. Ground that has been turned will certainly stay clean until the spring. Its nakedness is satisfying. The no-digging school are missing out on something besides the exercise. And it is wonderful how the frost really does break down those clayey clods.

Grass is growing only at a snail's pace (the snails themselves are in hibernation; I sometimes discover a hibernaculum in which they form large, inert clusters. Slugs, alas, are not such gentlemen). I don't believe in ever letting up on lawn mowing completely. If the air dries sufficiently to allow the dew to evaporate, as can happen beneath an overcast sky, we'll seize our opportunity to mow in any winter month. But it doesn't need to happen often.

The fact of the last leaves being off the trees and shrubs is a relief. The garden seems so much lighter, despite the sun's weakness and its infrequent appearances.

Large parts of the garden retain many beautiful features and effects. We sometimes need to re-train our eyes to see and appreciate them. This was brought strongly home to me after Pamla Toler's first of many visits, which was during a winter's fog. She spent hours in the garden; I couldn't imagine doing what. But she eventually came in, elated. She always seems to know

Opposite: Turban gourds, displayed in the porch.

183

when her efforts will turn out successfully. In fact they were triumphant. The topiary peacocks were used as endpapers in *The Englishman's Garden*. Skimmias in berry with the faintest outline of Dixter gable and roof looming in the background were used by the German magazine *Architektur und Wohnen*. There was another of evergreen ferns, *Blechnum chilense*, and of *Hebe* 'Mrs Winder', which is at its best in winter. And yet another of *Garrya elliptica* and *Daphniphyllum macropodum*, with the house hovering behind, both featuring in magazine publications.

One visit was during stormy weather on 19 and 20 December. It was pelting. I've never met another photographer who didn't reject such conditions utterly. Pamla Toler welcomes them. One of her pictures, looking across the Barn Garden towards the Oast House, had the spiky evergreen leaves of *Yucca gloriosa* 'Nobilis' and *Phormium cookianum* 'Tricolor' in the foreground. In the middle distance, a fountain from a single specimen of *Miscanthus sinensis* 'Variegatus', wherein the green and white striping had now changed to a warm straw that shows up especially well in rain. The barn roof tiles were wet and gleaming.

From the same position, with the yucca in the foreground, she turned her camera a little to the left so as to have the house in the background. The Sunk Garden pond was now in the middle distance, its water 'boiling' in the rain and wind. It is as exciting as a moving picture. Ghostly, upright spikes of pampas grass are on one side.

Then, turning the camera further leftwards still, the next picture looks along a flagstone path, itself gleaming in the wet and reflecting what light there is. To right and left are interesting plant shapes, greatest colour coming from two grasses, *Hakonechloa macra* 'Aureola', which is only a foot tall, and the 4-ft *Spartina michauxiana* 'Aureomarginata'. Both are yellow-variegated in their growing season but a pale, yet warm straw now.

At the end of this path, Pamla Toler took a photograph showing the value of dead hydrangea heads on the hortensia 'Vicomtesse de Vibraye'. They are warm brown and show up behind a pale fringe of the dwarf green-and-white bamboo, *Arundinaria variegata*. There are also the solid shapes of evergreen shrubs: *Olearia ilicifolia*, of a leaden colour, looks full of lively vitality because glistening in the wet. There is the pale green of *Pieris formosa* (slightly chlorotic on my soil), the darkness of *Osmanthus delavayi*, the bulk of a back-of-border *Eucryphia* × *intermedia*, while in the distance you see, beyond a yew hedge, the skeletal silhouette of a walnut tree's crown *(p. 186)*.

Everything being wet somehow looks very good. Gardeners are seldom deterred from showing their gardens to like-minded friends in the rain, and

Fog and foliage: *Hebe* 'Mrs Winder' and *Blechnum chilense*,
an evergreen fern from southern South America.

The Barn Garden on a wet day, with dead hydrangea heads and bamboo,
Arundinaria variegata, in front. Evergreens also contribute *(p. 184)*.

how right they are. One of my most memorable of many visits to Inverewe
Gardens in north-west Scotland was during two hours of non-stop rain. I
was with the right person and in the right mood. We enjoyed every minute.

But my borders' abiding strengths in winter, as revealed by these
photographs, are in their evergreens, in certain dried flower heads like
hydrangea, sedum and cardoon, and in the ornamental grasses. These last are
still underrated in our country but are much more used on the Continent – in
Germany especially – from where most of the newer varieties eventually
reach us. They turn to ethereal shades of warm brown and paler straw as the
sap gradually withdraws from stems and foliage. This only happens, to the
majority, in December.

Opposite: Miscanthus 'Silver Feather' stripped but pennons still flying *(p. 174)*.

Meanwhile there are flowers about. This is no mere dead month. Winter sweet, *Chimonanthus praecox*, is coming on apace. Chinese witch hazel, *Hamamelis mollis*, even if not yet flowering outside (though it will be by the month's last days), will open indoors with the minimum of forcing.

Before the first heavy frosts is usually the best moment for the winter cherry, *Prunus subhirtella* 'Autumnalis', of which I grow the faintly pink-flushed 'Rosea'. It's lovely to have it at this season, but if it flowered at any other we might be inclined to deride its wan ineffectiveness in the garden scene. However, picked in bud one can make quite a lot of it indoors. I think my tree will soon be killed by the enormously vigorous 'Paul's Himalayan Musk Rambler' growing through and over it. That flowers late in June, with cascades of double, pale pink blossom. Short though its season is, I get more of a kick from it than from the cherry.

The winter jasmine, *Jasminum nudiflorum*, is a more cheerful flower altogether. It has a long season but is usually at its most colourful in mid-December. Though it doesn't demand a wall, it is usually given one, and this certainly protects it a little from frost. The open flowers are distinctly frost-sensitive.

Frost on the lawns makes me wary of walking on them in that state. Every footprint leaves its legacy. So if I see anyone else walking on a frosted lawn I make a comment. 'Rose,' I said sharpish to Rose Barnes, who (thirty years ago) lived in the cottage at the bottom of the garden and came to wash up for us after lunch, 'if you walk on the grass you'll make it black.' 'The paths are so slippery. I'm afraid to break my leg,' said Rose. 'Well, if you're really afraid, I suppose you must walk on the grass,' said I, grudgingly. When she recounted this to my mother, Rose added, 'But I could see he'd rather I'd broke my leg!'

I'm only human – sometimes.

Index

Bold figures denote illustrations. In some cases there are also textual references on these pages.

Abelia × *grandiflora* 146
Abutilon: *A. megapotamicum* 146; *A.* × *suntense* 86
Acaena: *A. affinis* 140; *A. novae-zelandiae* 125
Achillea × *taygetea* 90, 175
Achnatherum calamagrostis **149**
aconite 46, 63; *A.* 'Ivorine' 98; *A.* 'Sparks' Variety' 91, 112
Adiantum 72
Ageratum houstonianum 152
Alchemilla 80, **81, 113**, 139
Allium: *A. christophii* 116, **117**, 138; *A. tuberosum* 138, 146
almond, dwarf 36, 68
Alnus cordata **45**, 55
Alstroemeria 91; *A. ligtu* 114, 153–4
Alyssum 64
Anagallis linifolia 153
Anemone 63; *A. appenina* 15; *A. blanda* 73; *A. hortensis* 21; Japanese 146, **147**; wood 16, 49
Anthemis tinctoria 116, 175
Anthericum liliago 96
apple 29; 'Bramley's Seedling' 79, 169; crab 11–12, 79–80
apricot 36
Aquilegia 178, 180
Aronia arbutifolia 'Erecta' **156**, 164
Artemisia: *A. arborescens* 147; *A. canescens* 151; *A. lactiflora* 138
artichokes 41, 59, 127
Arum: *A. creticum* 86, **87**; *A. italicum* 'Pictum' 25, 148
arum: dragon 124; lilies 21, 102
Arundinaria falconeri 98, **119**, **181, 186**
Arundo donax 125–6
Asclepias tuberosa **149**
ash 27, 29, 110, 171
Ashbee, John **28**, 177

aspen 160
Asperula odorata 72
Asphodeline liburnica 91, 123
Aster: *A. amellus* 'Violet Queen' 149, **150**; *A. ericoides* 'Esther' 163; *A. lateriflorus* 'Horizontalis' 162, **163**; *A. novae anglicae* 'Alma Potschke' 151; *A. pappei* 158; *A. sedifolius* 91, 138
Astilbe taquetii **119**
Astrantia 'Sunningdale Variegated' 84
Aubrieta **32**, 64
Aucuba 34, 66; *A. japonica* 'Crotonifolia' 174
auricula 180
azalea 73
Azara: *A. microphylla* 68; *A. serrata* 88

bamboo 59–60, **78**, 98, 168–9, **181**, 184, **186**
Baptisia australis 98
Barn Garden **2**, 11–12, **30**, 68, 72, **89**, 124, 126, 129–30, 137, 146, 151, 164, **165**, **170**, 184, **186**
Barnes, Rose 188
bay laurel 9, 80, 166
beech 71
begonias 148
Bellis 180
Berberis thunbergii 'Gold Ring' 148
Bergenia (*Megasea*) *cordifolia* 13
berries 34, 39, 154, 160–61, 175–7
birch 160
Blechnum chilense 184, **185**
bloodroot, Canadian 71
bluebells 64
borders 25, 138–40, 158, **179**, 186; see also Long Border
Bowles's golden sedge 102
Briza maxima 126
broccoli, purple sprouting 42
Brodiaea laxa 180
broom 86, 100, **108**, 111–12

Buddleia 59, 145; *B. auriculata* 167
Buphthalmum speciosum **111**, 112
buttercups 89

cabbage 41–2
Calamagrostis acutiflora 'Stricta' 126, 166
Calceolaria: *C. integrifolia* 151; *C. mexicana* 152
Calluna vulgaris 16
Caltha polypetala **62**
Camassia 127; *C. esculenta* 90, 177; *C. leichtlinii* 177
Campanula poscharskyana 66; *C. lactiflora* 'Prichard's Variety' 113; *C. persicifolia* 116; *C. portenschlagiana* 68
campion 98
Canna 91, 134
Cardamine hirsuta 48
cardoon 84, **137**, 138, 186
Carex stricta 'Aurea' 102
carnation 180
carrot 40
Castanea sativa: see chestnut
catkins 25, 38, **45**, 55
Ceanothus 59, 158
celandine 48, **49**
Celastrus orbiculatus **23**, 162, **163**, 174
celeriac 40, 169
Centaurea gymnocarpa 158
Ceratostigma 148
Cestrum parqui 138
Chaerophyllum hirsutum 'Roseum' 86
Chamaecyparis: 'Ellwood's Gold' 29; 'Ericoides' **42**, 181
cherry: bush 68, 160, 188; morello 36
chestnut: *Castanea sativa* 'Albomarginata' 116; horse 75
chicory 43, 169
Chimonanthus praecox 22, 23, 24, 173–4, 188
chives 43, 83; see also *Allium*
Choisya ternata 88
Chrysanthemum 134

Chusquea culeou **78**, 169
chutney, tomato 154–5
Cimicifuga ramosa 'Atropurpurea' **137**, 147
Cistus 59, 158; *C. cyprius* 123–4
Clematis 25; *C. cirrhosa balearica* 34, **35**; *C. montana* 88; *C.* × *jackmanii* 'Superba' **111**, 112, 114; *C.* × *jouiniana* 'Praecox' 124; *C. recta* 83, 91, 113
Cleome spinosa 152
Clerodendrum bungei 145–6
clover, red 90
Colchicum 48, 140, **150**, 151
columbine 82, 178
comfrey, 84, 148
Convolvulus: *C. cneorum* 59; *C. mauritanicus* 59, 130, 158
cornflower 141
Cornus alba 39, **62**, **74**, 147, 162, 174
Cortaderia selloana 'Pumila' 164, **165**
Cosmos bipinnatus 152, 153
Cotinus coggygria 114, 115
Cotoneaster horizontalis 161, 171, **176**
Crambe cordifolia 84
cranesbills **97**, 102, 160
Crataegus 37; *C. prunifolia* **161**
Crathes Castle Gardens 122
creeping jenny 87
Crinum × *powellii* 102
Crocosmia: *C. masonorum* 'Dixter Flame' **135**, 136; *C.* 'Solfatare' 149
Crocus 33, 50–51, 140, 177; *C. aureus* 33; *C. chrysanthus* 33; *C. c.* 'Snow Bunting' 33; *C. nudiflorus* **150**, 151; *C. speciosus* 66, 151, 166; *C. tomasinianus* 33, 66
cucumber 155
Cuphea: *C. cyanea* 131; *C. miniata* 'Firefly' 152–3
Cupressus sempervirens 55
currants, red and black 47, 127
cyclamen 166; *C. hederifolium* (*neapolitanum*) 66, 151–2

Cymbalaria muralis 81
Cynara cardunculus 84, **137**, 138
Cynoglossum amabile 141
Cyperus longus 162
Cytisus: C. fragrans 21, 73; *C. praecox* 86

Dactylorhiza fuchsii 102
daffodil: *see Narcissus*
daisy 81–2, 98, 112, 114, 144–5; *Bellis* **111**, 180; Mexican 81; michaelmas 162–3; moon 90, **103**: *see also Aster*
Danaë racemosa 66
Daphne 36, 87; *D. mezereum* 54, 55
Daphniphyllum macropodum 25, 164, 184
Darmera peltata **62**, 63
Davallia mariesii 72
delphinium 91, 98
Dianthus 180–81; *D. barbatus* 82, 133, 180; 'Queen of Hearts' 141, 181; 'Rainbow Loveliness' 141, 180–81
Diascia 59; **117**
Dierama pulcherrimum 126
digging, winter 26, 177, 183
Digitalis 178
Dixter, Great: *house 7–9; Great Hall 8,* **23**, 174; Yeoman's Hall 8–9, 109; views **8**, **14**, **19**, **28**, **89**, **139**, 164, 169, 184; nursery 16–17, 58, 90, 106, 157–8
Dixter, Little 7, 17
dogwood: *see Cornus*
doronicum 82, 178
Dracunculus vulgaris 124
ducks and duckweed 76, 79

Echinacea purpurea **139**
Elaeagnus 100; *E. pungens* 'Maculata' 84, 177
elder 47, 107, **111**, 112
elderflower cordial, 107
elm, 'Dickson's Golden' 53, 83, 115
Elodea 101; *E. canadensis* 40; *E. crispa* 39–40
Eremurus: E. bungei 98; *E. robustus* 84, **85**
Erigeron: E. glaucus 82; *E. mucronatus* 81
Eryngium: E. giganteum 126; *E.* × *oliverianum* **117**, **123**; *E. pandanifolium* 167–8
Erysimum: 'Bowles's Mauve' 59, 178–9; *E. linifolium* 179

Eyrthronium dens-canis 52, **53**
Escallonia: E. bifida **144**, 145; *E. virgata* 126; *E.* 'Iveyi' 110–11
Eucryphia: × *intermedia* 184, **186**; 'Nymansay' 130
Euonymus fortunei 25, 83
Eupatorium 146
Euphorbia 94, 160; *E. griffithii* 'Fireglow' 86; *E. palustris* 25, 71, 84; *E. robbiae* 64, **65**

Fatsia japonica 135, 146, 174
Felicia 21, 59; *F. amelloides* 131, 158
ferns 25, 72, **73**, 76, 90, 98, 135, 148, 175, 184, **185**
fertilizers 37, 47, 59, 127, 130, 140; *see also* mulching fig 9, 36–7, 141, 172
Filipendula rubra 'Venusta' 127
Fish, Margery 32, 71, 96, 112, 165
fish 60, 131, 133
forget-me-nots 71, 83
foxgloves 82
Fritillaria: F. imperialis 48; *F. meleagris* 15, **61**, 63; *F. pallidiflora* 72–3
Fuchsia 21, 25, 51, 59, 158; 'Mme Cornelissen' 164; 'Mrs Popple' 146; 'Riccartoni' 146; 'Versicolor' 126

Galanthus 31, 51, 63; *G. ikariae latifolius* 51; 'Hippolyta' 32; *G. nivalis* 'Atkinsii' 25; *G. n.* 'Samuel Arnott' **32**; *G. n.* reginae-algae 51; *G. platyphyllus* 51
Garrya elliptica 25, 184
gazanias 21, 59, 158
Genista 21, 73; *G. aetnensis* 111–12; *G. lydia* 158; *G. tenera (virgata)* 100, **108**
Gentiana asclepiadea 148
Geranium: G. dalmaticum 68; *G. endressii* 'A.T. Johnson' **97**, 98; *G. himalayense (grandiflorum)* 97; *G. maculatum* 86; *G. maderense* 134–5; *G. pratense* 102, **108**; 'Russell Prichard' **98**; **108**; *G. wallichianum* 'Buxton's Blue' 154
'geraniums' 21, 66, 130, **131**
Geum 82; *G. rivale* 71
Gladiolus byzantinus 83, 102; *G. segetum* 102; *G. tristis* 21, 73, 141
Gleditsia triacanthos 114
globe flower 86, **87**, 177–8

Glyceria maxima 39
gooseberries 47, 91, 127
gorse 16
gourds 155, **182**
grass 126–7, 140, **150**, 151, 177, 183
grasses 80–81, 89, 103, 126, 127, 166; ornamental 60, 125–6, 135, **179**, 186; pampas 164, **165**, 184
Great Dixter: *see* Dixter, Great
greenhouse 21–2, 157–8
Grigson, Jane 91
Gunnera **61**, 62–3; *G. manicata*, 62, 76, **77**; *G. tinctoria*, 62
Gymnocarpium dryopteris 72

Hakonechloa macra 'Aureola' **166**, 184
Hamamelis mollis 22, 188
haresfoot, creeping 72
hawthorn 37, 47, **161**
heather 16
Hebe 158; 'Boughton Dome' 93–4; 'Mrs Winder' 184, **185**
Hedera cancariensis 'Variegata' 164
hedges 26, 47; *see also* yew
Hedychium 91
Helenium 'Moerheim Beauty' 114, **115**
Helianthemum 158
Helianthus salicifolius 116
Helichrysum 158; *H. microphyllum* 130; *H. petiolatum* 21, 22, 130, **131**, 151; *H. splendidum* **42**, 94
heliotrope 131; winter 24
hellebore **26**, 33–4, 66
Hemerocallis: H. flava 139; 'Marion Vaughan' 112
Hesperis matronalis 178
Hidcote Manor 51
High Garden **11**, **50**, 89, 93–8, 133, 136, 151
holly 176–7
honesty 86, 178
honeysuckle: *see Lonicera*
Horse Pond 16, 39–40, 49–50, 53, 60, 62, 64, **74**, 79, 100, **101**, 102, 127, **128**, 129, 140, 151, **159**, 160, 162
Hosta 84, 148; 'Honeybells' 148; *H. lancifolia* 146; 'Royal Standard' 148; *H. sieboldiana* 'Elegans' 80, 98; 'Tall Boy' 124; *H. ventricosa* 'Aureomarginata' 112
Hottonia palustris 162
hyacinth 54

Hydrangea 93, **117–20**, 121–2; care 47, 58, 158; 'Ayesha' **136**, 137; 'Blue Wave' 121–2; 'Blue Bird' **118**, 121–2; 'Floribunda' 138; 'Générale Vicomtesse de Vibraye' **119**, 121–2; 'Geoffrey Chadbund' **120**, 121; 'Grayswood' 121; 'Hamburg' 121, **145**; 'Hidcote' 121; 'Mme Emile Mouillière' 121–2, **145**, 146; 'Mariesii' **137**; *H. paniculata* 138; *H. petiolaris* 121, 145, 164; 'Preziosa' 116, **117**; 'Tardiva' 138; 'Veitchii' 121; *H. villosa* 130; 'Westfalen' **118**, 121; in winter 164, 172, **179**, 184, **186**

ilex: *I. altaclarensis* 'Golden King' 176–7; oak 102–3
Ingram, Collingwood ('Cherry') 52, 55, 68, 71
Inula magnifica 112
Inverewe Gardens 186
Iris 19, **73**; bearded 11–12, 66; Dutch 180; *I. bucharica* **73**; *I. danfordiae* 20; *I. histroides* 'Major' 19, 20; *I. laevigata* 'Zambesi' 143; *I. pseudacorus* 76, 100–101; *I. sibirica* 96; *I. versicolor* 101; *I. winogradowii* **20**
ivy 29, 39, 164

Jacob's ladder 86
jasmine: *J. officinale* × 'Affine' 130; winter 175, 188
Juniperus sabina tamariscifolia 181

Kaa, Romke van de 24, 49
kingcups **62**, 63
Kirengeshoma palmata 148
Kniphofia: K. caulescens 148; *K. rooperi* 165–6; *K. uvaria* 'Nobilis' **138**

lady's mantle: *see Alchemilla*
lady's smock 16, 63
Lamium maculatum 'White Nancy' 84
Lathraea clandestine 53
laurel, bay 9, 80, 166
laurustinus **42**
Lavatera olbia 124, 158
lavender 158, 162
lawns 46, 73, 83, 89, 183, 188
leek 41
Lemna 79
lettuce 42–3, 45, 127, 169

Leucojum: *L. aestivum* 33, 64;
  L. a. 'Gravetye Giant' 64, **74;**
  L. autumnale 151; *L. vernum*
  32–3
lichen **69**, 73
Ligularia doria 114
Ligustrum: *L. quihoui* **145**, 146;
  L. × vicaryi 112, 174
lilac: *see Syringa*
Lilium formosanum **142**, 152
lily: arum 21, 102; day 112; foxtail
  84, **85**, 98; Kaffir **175**; Lent 15,
  49–50, 63; Scarborough 152;
  torch 138, 148, 165–6; of the
  valley 96
Linum grandiflorum 'Rubrum'
  153
Liriope muscari **150**, 151
Lobelia cardinalis 102
London Pride 96
Long Border 13, 46–7, 53, 80,
  82, 83, 84, 93, **108**, 110–12,
  113, 114, **115**, 116, **117**, 133,
  135, 137, 147, **153**, 154, 162–
  8, 176
Lonicera 24, 88, 124; *L. ×*
  americana 113; *L. fragrantissima*
  24; *L. japonica* 'Halliana' 24; *L.*
  × purpusii 174
Lotus corniculatus 125
Lunaria annua 86, 178
lupin 82, 91, **92, 94**, 95, 178
Lychnis: *L. chalcedonica* 91, **115**:
  L. coronaria 126
Lysichitum americanum 76
Lysimachia: *L. nummularia*
  'Aurea' 87; *L. punctata* 102

Magnolia 33–4, 175, **176**; *M.*
  denudata 66; *M. kobus* 65; *M.*
  liliflora 'Nigra' 27; *M. ×*
  loebneri 'Leonard Messel' 65;
  M. soulangiana 'Lennei' **14, 67**;
  M. stellata 64–5; *M. × veitchii*
  'Peter Veitch' 66
Mahonia 60; *M. × media* **168**; *M.*
  × undulata **181**
mallow: *Malope trifida* 136, 152,
  153; tree 124
Malus 11–12, 79–80
marigolds 133; African 152
Massingham, Betty 13
meadow sweet 127
medlar 172, **173**
Melandrium rubrum 'Flore
  Pleno' 98
Melianthus major **134**
mignonette 131
Miscanthus sinensis 46;
  'Gracillimus' 166; 'Silver

Feather' 166, **174, 187**;
  'Strictus' 166, **181**;
  'Variegatus' **135**, 166, **170**,
  184
Moat, Lower **45**, 76, 79, 172
Moat, Upper **14**, 15, 64, 127,
  150, 151
Molinia caerulea 166
Monarda 90, 102, **108**;
  'Cambridge Scarlet' 112–13
monkshood 46, 63, 91, 98, 112
Montbretia 149
mulberry 112, 171
mulching 37, 53, 59, 172
mullein 114, 133, 178
Mutisia oligodon 122
Myosotis 83
Myrtus communis 130

Narcissus 13, 15, 49, **50**, 51,
  57–8, 66, 72, 179; 'Barrii
  conspicuus' **56**; 'Emperor' **56**;
  N. minor **53**, 54; *N. poeticus* 15,
  90; *N. pseudonarcissus* 15, 49–
  50, 63; 'Tête-à-Tête' **50**, 54;
  'Tittle Tattle' 179
Nasturtium 138, 166
Nemophila maculata 83
Nerine × bowdenii 149, **150**, 166
Nicotiana sylvestris 152, 153

oak: *see Quercus*
oast house 9, **30**, 79, 88, **170**,
  184
Oenothera stricta 124
Olearia ilicifolia 184, **186**
Omphalodes cappadocica **70**, 71,
  82
Ophioglossum vulgatum 90
orange: Mexican 88; mock 124
orchard 13, 15, 90, 100, 103;
  daffodils 50, 56, 57–8
Orchard Garden 154, 168
orchid: *O. mascula* 15, **63**; *O.*
  morio 90; spotted 63, 102
Osmanthus delavayi 12, 68, 158,
  184, **186**
Osmunda 76
Osteospermum 59, 158; *O.*
  jucundum 98
Oxalis rubra 146
oxygenators 39–40, 133

pansies 82, 180
Papaver: *P. bracteata* 'Goliath'
  97; *P. orientale* **95**; *P. heldreichii*
  96
parsley 45
parsnip 41
Paulownia 66

paving, plants in 48, 51, 80–82,
  102, 148
peach 53–6
pear 79, 93, 94, 144; wild 9, **10**,
  78, 79, 172, **176**
Peltiphyllum peltatum **62**, 63
Penstemon 158; 'Drinkstone
  Red' 113
peony 54–5, 96
periwinkle 68, 166–7
Phalaris arundinacea 'Picta' 102
pheasant's eye 90
Philadelphus 124
Phlomis fruticosa 114
Phlox 46, **108**, 114, 139–40; *P.*
  douglasii 87; 'Mia Ruys' **108**;
  P. paniculata 91, 112
Phormium cookianum **170**, 184
Phyllostachys nigra 168–9
Pieris formosa 184, **186**
Pileostegia viburnoides **145**, 146
Pinus patula 103, 166
Plumbago 148
plums 140–41
Polemonium 'Lambrook Mauve'
  86
Polyanthus 15, 175, 179–80
Polygonum vaccinifolium 163
Polystichum setiferum 72
poppy 76, 84, **95**, 96, **97**
pots, ornamental 72, **73**, 91,
  130, 152
primrose 64, 76, 124
privet 112, **145**, 146, 174
propagation 45–6, 59, 90, 141,
  153–4, 157–8, 171–2
pruning: bamboo 59–60, 98; *fruit*
  36, 47; hydrangea 47; rose 27, 28;
  shrubs 25–6, 27, 54, 110
Prunus: *P. glandulosa* 'Alba
  Plena' 68, 160; *P. subhirtella*
  'Autumnalis' **188**; *P. tenella*
  'Firehill' 68

Quercus 16, 74, 75–6, 129, 172;
  Q. ilex 102–3; *Q. rubra* 60, 98,
  100

Ranunculus: *R. aconitifolius*
  'Flore Pleno' 86, **87**; *R.*
  auricomus 16; *R. ficaria* 48, **49**
raspberry 47, 127, 154
Rhododendron 16, 53, 55, 72, 73,
  172; 'Cynthia' 76; *R. dauricum*
  55; *R. × loderi* 'King George'
  72; *R. obtusum* 'Amoenum' 72;
  R. praecox 55; *R. praevernum*
  55; 'Tessa' 55
rhubarb 90–91

Rodgersia pinnata 'Suberba' 84
Rose Garden 80, **104**, 105–6,
  136
roses: *care 27, 28,* 48, 96; hips
  80, 154; repeat flowering 140;
  'Canary Bird' 80; *R.*
  cantabrigiensis 80; 'Candeur
  Lyonnaise' 105; 'Chapeau de
  Napoléon' 116; 'Crested
  Moss' 116; 'Eastea's Golden
  Rambler' 105; 'The Fairy' 138,
  140; 'Felicia' 97; 'Florence
  May Morse' **108**; 112;
  'Fruehlingsgold' 95; 'Mme
  Butterfly' 106; 'Mme Isaac
  Pereire' **105**, 140; 'Mrs Oakley
  Fisher' 105; *R. moyesii* 154;
  'Paul's Himalayan Musk
  Rambler' 188; *R.*
  pimpinellifolia 80; *R. pinnata*
  'Superba', 84; *R. primula* 80;
  R. rugosa 'Alba' 154; *R. sancta*
  95–6; *R. setipoda* 154
rowan 160
Royal Horticultural Society 48,
  88, 166–7
Rubus: *R. tricolor* 98; *R.*
  pheonicolasius 154
Rudbeckia **147**, 148
Rumex scutatus 48

Sage, Jerusalem 114
salads 42–3, 45, 48, 127, 169
Salix **62**; *S. alba* 'Argentea' 53,
  115; *S. caprea* 53–4; *S.*
  daphnoides 'Aglaia' **38**, 39; *S.*
  hastata 'Wehrhahnii' 71; *S.*
  sachalinensis 'Sekka' 54
salsify 41
Salvia **115**; *S. nemorosa* 90; *S.*
  patens 91; 'Cambridge Blue'
  154
Sambucus: *S. nigra* 47, 107; *S.*
  racemosa 'Plumosa Aurea' **111**,
  112
Sanguinaria canadensis 71
Sarcococca 24
savory 158
saxifrage **62**, 63, 68; *S. fortunei*
  166; *S. × umbrosa* 96
scabious, sweet 141
Schisandra rubriflora 88, 162
Schizophragma integrifolium 121,
  122, 145
Schizostylis coccinea 102, 148,
  175
scorzonera 41
scilla: *S. bifolia* 51; *S. bithynica*
  51, **52, 66**; *S. sibirica* 51, 52; *S.*
  verna 51

sculpture, garden 13, 103
Sedum 117, 186; 'Ruby Glow'
  138; *S. spectabile* 138
Selinum carvifolium 96
Senecio: S. cineraria 158; *S.*
  leucostachys 158; *S. pulcher* 149;
  S. smithii 102, 149; *S.*
  tanguticus 174
Serratula seoanei 175
shallot 40
Sheffield Park 73, 76, 160, 168
Sissinghurst Castle 7–8, 68, 105
Sisyrinchium angustifolium 80–81
Skimmia japonica 34–5, 164, 184
skunk cabbage 76
smoke bush 115
Smyrnium perfoliatum 86
snake, grass 60, 124
snowdrop: *see Galanthus*
snowflake: *see Leucojum*
Sorbus 37; *S.* × *hostii* 154; *S.*
  'Joseph Rock' 160; *S.*
  meliosmifolia 47
sorrel 48
Spartina michauxiana
  'Aureomarginata' 184
speedwell, ivy 37
spindle berries 174
Spiraea japonica 'Goldflame' 70,
  71
sprouts, brussels 41
stocks 82, 178
Stratiotes aloides 133
sunflower 116

Sunk Garden 10–11, 30, 68,
  125–6, 181, 184; fish 131, 133;
  irises 101, 143; pots 91, 130,
  131
supports, plant 27, 91, 138, 141
sweet pea 45
sweet rocket 178
sweet william 82, 133, 180
Symphytum × *uplandicum* 84,
  148
Syringa 16, 32, 76, 87–8;
  'Souvenir de Louis Spaeth' 76,
  88

Tagetes 133
Tamarisk ramosissima (T.
  petandra) 115, 135, 136–7
tarragon 48
teasel 136
Telekia speciosa 111, 112
terrace 14, 67, 91, 126, 130
Thalictrum aquilegifolium 96
Thermopsis 86
thistles, sow 107
Thuja occidentalis 'Rheingold'
  29, 181
thyme 87, 158
Tithonia rotundifolia 152
toadflax, ivy-leaved 81
tomato 154–5
toothwort 53
topiary 10, 14, 19, 85, 132, 139,
  162, 169, 177, 184
trefoil, birdsfoot 125

Trollius 'Canary Bird' 86, 87,
  177–8
Tropaeolum: T. magnus 166; *T.*
  tricolorum 21; *T. tuberosum* 166,
  167
Tulipa (dachshund) 17, 43, 130,
  143, 155, 157, 161
tulip 47, 179, 180; 'Dyanito' 82;
  T. eichleri 180; *T. kaufmannia*
  51; 'Mrs John Scheepers' 82;
  'Orange Emperor' 68;
  'Orange Favourite' 83; *T.*
  sprengeri 51; *T. sylvestris* 51
Typha latifolia 39

Vallota speciosa 152
vegetables 40–43, 59, 90, 93,
  106, 127, 140, 169
Veratrum album 124, 125
Verbascum: V. chaixii 114; *V.*
  olympicum 132, 133, 178
Verbena 158; *V. bonariensis* 135,
  136–7, 145–6
Veronica 115; *V. gentianoides* 87
Viburnum: V. × *bodnantense* 175;
  V. farreri 175; *V. opulus*
  'Compactum' 27, 162
Vicia: V. cracca 127; *V. sepia* 125
Vinca: V. difformis 166–7; *V.*
  major 'Alba' 66
Viola 180; *V. cornuta* 'Alba' 80,
  81, 82, 113; 'Maggie Mott' 106
violet 48, 52–3; water 40, 162
Viscaria 141

Wakehurst Place 103
Wall Garden 93, 123, 124,
  146
wallflower 73, 82, 171, 178–9
walls 10; plants in 34, 64, 68,
  94, 146; *see also* paving
walnut 184, 186
water gardening 16, 39–40, 62,
  76, 79, 101–2, 133, 162
watering system 106
waterlilies 39, 40, 100, 102
weedkiller 37, 40, 48, 101, 125
Weigela florida 'Variegata' 116
whitebeam 154
wild gardening 13, 15–16, 62–
  4, 86, 89, 102; *see also* grass
willow: *see Salix*
willowherb, lesser 107
wineberries, Japanese 154
winter sweet: *see Chimonanthus*
wisteria 88, 89
witch hazel 173; Chinese 22,
  23, 188
woodruff 72
Woodwardia radicans 175

yew 11, 38, 55, 103; hedges 10,
  15, 26, 37, 79, 158, 166, 177;
  see also topiary
Yucca gloriosa 11–12, 124, 170,
  184

Zantedeschia aethiopica 21, 102
Zephyranthes candida 151

---◆---

Illustration Acknowledgements

The author and publishers are grateful to Pamla Toler and Impact Photos for permission to reproduce the photographs on the following pages: frontispiece, 18, 23, 26, 28 *(top left, top right, bottom)*, 30, 41, 49, 50, 56, 61, 62 *(top left)*, 65, 69, 70, 73, 77, 81, 83, 85, 87, 94, 97, 99, 103, 104, 105, 111, 113, 115, 117 *(top and bottom)*, 118, 120, 125, 128, 132, 135 *(bottom left)*, 137, 139, 142, 147, 159, 163 *(top left)*, 165, 170, 174, 179, 181, 182, 185, 186, 187; and to Olive Cook for photographs by Edwin Smith on pages 8 and 14. All other photographs were taken by or are the property of Christopher Lloyd. The plan on page 6 was drawn by Eugene Fleury, based on a survey by Martina Jordan, John Lucas and Guy Bartley (Landscape Architects).